S. Hrg. 115–150

DOUBLING DOWN ON INDIAN GAMING: EXAMINING NEW ISSUES AND OPPORTUNITIES FOR SUCCESS IN THE NEXT 30 YEARS

HEARING

BEFORE THE

COMMITTEE ON INDIAN AFFAIRS UNITED STATES SENATE

ONE HUNDRED FIFTEENTH CONGRESS

FIRST SESSION

OCTOBER 4, 2017

Printed for the use of the Committee on Indian Affairs

U.S. GOVERNMENT PUBLISHING OFFICE

28–581 PDF   WASHINGTON : 2018

For sale by the Superintendent of Documents, U.S. Government Publishing Office
Internet: bookstore.gpo.gov Phone: toll free (866) 512–1800; DC area (202) 512–1800
Fax: (202) 512–2104 Mail: Stop IDCC, Washington, DC 20402–0001

COMMITTEE ON INDIAN AFFAIRS

JOHN HOEVEN, North Dakota, *Chairman*
TOM UDALL, New Mexico, *Vice Chairman*

JOHN BARRASSO, Wyoming	MARIA CANTWELL, Washington
JOHN MCCAIN, Arizona	JON TESTER, Montana,
LISA MURKOWSKI, Alaska	AL FRANKEN, Minnesota
JAMES LANKFORD, Oklahoma	BRIAN SCHATZ, Hawaii
STEVE DAINES, Montana	HEIDI HEITKAMP, North Dakota
MIKE CRAPO, Idaho	CATHERINE CORTEZ MASTO, Nevada
JERRY MORAN, Kansas	

T. MICHAEL ANDREWS, *Majority Staff Director and Chief Counsel*
JENNIFER ROMERO, *Minority Staff Director and Chief Counsel*

CONTENTS

	Page
Hearing held on October 4, 2017	1
Statement of Senator Cantwell	3
Statement of Senator Heitkamp	19
Statement of Senator Hoeven	1
Statement of Senator Udall	2

WITNESSES

Chaudhuri, Hon. Jonodev Osceola, Chairman, National Indian Gaming Commission	4
Prepared statement	6
Escalanti, Hon. Keeny, President, Fort Yuma Quechan Indian Tribe	23
Prepared statement	24
Forsman, Hon. Leonard, Chairman, Suquamish Tribe	31
Prepared statement	33
Frank, Hon. Harold "Gus", Chairman, Forest County Potawatomi Community	27
Prepared statement	29
Stevens, Jr., Ernest L., Chairman, National Indian Gaming Association	36
Prepared statement	38
Tahsuda, III, John, Principal Deputy Assistant Secretary, Indian Affairs, U.S. Department of the Interior	12
Prepared statement	14

APPENDIX

Allen, Hon. W. Ron, Tribal Chairman/CEO, Jamestown S'Klallam Tribe, prepared statement	55
Cowan. Klint A., Shareholder, Fellers Snider, prepared statement	58
Response to written questions submitted by Hon. Jerry Moran to Hon. Jonodev Osceola Chaudhuri	59
Response to written questions submitted by Hon. Tom Udall to John Tahsuda III	61

DOUBLING DOWN ON INDIAN GAMING: EXAMINING NEW ISSUES AND OPPORTUNITIES FOR SUCCESS IN THE NEXT 30 YEARS

WEDNESDAY, OCTOBER 4, 2017

U.S. SENATE,
COMMITTEE ON INDIAN AFFAIRS,
Washington, DC.

The Committee met, pursuant to notice, at 2:45 p.m. in room 216, Hart Senate Office Building, Hon. John Hoeven, Chairman of the Committee, presiding.

OPENING STATEMENT OF HON. JOHN HOEVEN, U.S. SENATOR FROM NORTH DAKOTA

The CHAIRMAN. Good afternoon. We will call this hearing to order.

Today, the Committee will examine new issues and opportunities in Indian gaming.

The tribal gaming industry has changed significantly since President Reagan signed the Indian Gaming Regulatory Act into law. The National Indian Gaming Commission recently announced that tribal gaming brought in $31.2 billion in gross gaming revenue for 2016, the largest amount in the history of Indian gaming. This is critical funding for essential and necessary tribal government services.

On July 22, 2015, the Committee last held an oversight hearing which involved the GAO study on Indian gaming regulation. Today, cyber security hacks, human trafficking, safety and security take the headlines at Indian gaming facilities. For example, in 2015, nearly 85,000 customers' personal data was compromised at the Firekeepers Casino in Battle Creek, Michigan as hackers accessed customer credit and debit card information.

Just last week, at the Committee hearing on human trafficking, witnesses noted that these despicable activities occurred at Indian casinos. For example, in my home State of North Dakota, the U.S. Attorney's office successfully prosecuted an adult predator who had been running a sex trafficking operation out of the Four Bears Casino in New Town, North Dakota.

This individual was sentenced to 45 years in prison or sex trafficking, sexual abuse and drug trafficking. In an interview with investigators, one of the victims disclosed that she had been sold for sex multiple times at the Four Bears Casino.

I look forward to hearing from our witnesses on how these types of threats and criminal activities are prevented or addressed, as well as other new issues and opportunities in the tribal gaming industry.

Before turning to the witnesses, I would again ask the Vice Chairman for his opening statement.

STATEMENT OF HON. TOM UDALL, U.S. SENATOR FROM NEW MEXICO

Senator UDALL. Thank you, Chairman Hoeven. Thank you for holding today's oversight hearing to discuss Indian gaming.

Before I address today's agenda, I want to convey my grief and sadness of the mass shooting that occurred in Las Vegas on Sunday night. My heart goes out to all the victims and their families. I know many tribal members were in Las Vegas on that night to attend a global gaming expo. My thoughts and prayers are with all the victims of this terrible and inexcusable tragedy.

For today's hearing, I hope that we recognize the achievements of the Indian Gaming Regulatory Act and also look ahead to the challenges confronting tribes that must compete in a constantly evolving economy with emerging technologies in the industry. Importantly, we must look ahead for future opportunities for tribes. We have seen Indian gaming make great impacts for tribes in the 29 years since Congress IGRA. I am honored to serve alongside one of the architects of that Act, Senator John McCain.

Senator McCain worked with my uncle, Mo Udall, who led the legislative effort on the House side. Together, they ushered in a new era for tribal self determination with a law that continues to provide economic opportunities to Indian Country that, prior to its passage, were unimaginable.

Senator McCain and Uncle Mo's efforts to pass this landmark legislation were a true showing of bipartisanship, one we need to see more of today.

Indian gaming has stood the test of time as a proven economic driver. Consider this, when Congress passed IGRA in 1988, gaming revenues were measured by the tens of millions. Nearly 30 years later, revenues are over $31 billion. Tribal enterprises can have a transformative effect by promoting tribal self sufficiency and strong tribal governments.

As Chairman Forsman of the Suquamish Tribe, will testify, the revenue flowing from gaming activities not only creates jobs and stimulates tribal economy, but also goes a long way to supplement the massive shortfalls left by the Federal Government's failure to appropriate adequate funding to meet Indian Country's needs. Unlike commercial casinos that generate revenue for shareholders, gaming revenue provides essential government services for tribal citizens, services like housing, health care, education, public safety and general social services.

The benefits of Indian gaming also go beyond reservation boundaries. According to the National Indian Gaming Association, tribal gaming has created nearly 700,000 jobs and generated more than $10 billion in revenue for Federal, State and local governments in 2015 alone.

Gaming revenue also supports tribal economic sovereignty. I have seen firsthand the impacts of gaming for the 15 tribes in New Mexico that operate gaming facilities. Tribes use gaming revenues to leverage and invest in new and diversified businesses from hotels to wineries. Tribes are launching and acquiring enterprises and industries that run the gamut from technology and advanced manufacturing to commercial real estate.

This durable economic cycle from gaming generated seed money to the diversified economic portfolios and strengthened tribal governments is one that we should look to help, not hinder.

While the benefits of gaming revenue to tribal governments are significant and have been the key to revitalizing some tribal economies, it is not the panacea for all. In fact, most tribes are not gaming tribes. Of the 567 federally-recognized Indian tribes, only 246 operate gaming facilities. Of those facilities, fewer still generate enough revenue to significantly reduce poverty rates in Indian Country that go beyond the national average.

There is still much work to be done to truly achieve tribal self determination and sufficiency. Indian gaming is certainly not the end of the story. What does the future of Indian gaming and IGRA hold? What is the next chapter?

I look forward to hearing how our witnesses answer those questions. It is clear to me that we, in Congress, must continue to work towards IGRA's goals, to foster tribal economic development, tribal self sufficiency and strong tribal governments.

Thank you, Mr. Chairman. I look forward to today's testimony.

The CHAIRMAN. Thank you, Vice Chairman Udall.

I, too, want to express my concern and prayers for all impacted by the terrible tragedy in Las Vegas.

I would also turn to Senator Cantwell for any opening statement she might have.

STATEMENT OF HON. MARIA CANTWELL, U.S. SENATOR FROM WASHINGTON

Senator CANTWELL. Thank you, Mr. Chairman. Thank you for the opportunity.

I want to say that I want to introduce the second panel and Chairman Forsman from the Suquamish Tribe. He has been the chairman since 2005 and has overseen, as my colleague just said, some economic and cultural revitalization of that tribe. We so appreciate him being here to testify today.

Under his leadership, it has grown as mentioned in the Ranking Member's testimony, as a vital employer in the region, gaming, seafood, construction, retail, entertainment. We appreciate the diversification. He is also an archeologist by training and was appointed by the last Administration as a tribal representative to our Advisory Council on Historic Preservation.

Last year, I had the privilege of being there as he was sworn in as the first Native American to serve on that Advisory Council as Vice Chairman. This past September, he was elected to the Affiliated Tribes of the Northwest which represents 57 different tribes from Alaska to California, Idaho, Nevada, Montana, Oregon and Washington. I know we will hear a lot from him on the second panel.

Thank you for allowing me to say a few words about him as we move through our witnesses today.

The CHAIRMAN. Thank you, Senator.

On our first panel, we will hear from The Honorable Jonodev Osceola Chaudhuri, Chairman, National Indian Gaming Commission in Washington, D.C. and also from Mr. John Tahsuda, Principal Deputy Assistant Secretary, Indian Affairs, U.S. Department of the Interior.

Please proceed.

STATEMENT OF HON. JONODEV OSCEOLA CHAUDHURI, CHAIRMAN, NATIONAL INDIAN GAMING COMMISSION

Mr. CHAUDHURI. Thank you, Chairman Hoeven, Vice Chairman Udall and members of the Committee, for inviting me to testify today. It is an honor to appear before you as Chairman of the National Indian Gaming Commission.

[Greeting in Native tongue.]

Mr. CHAUDHURI. Greetings and may Creator bless us today and Muscogee Creek.

All of the NIGC's hearts were broken on Sunday by the pointless, monstrous, mass shooting in Las Vegas. I cannot begin to comprehend the pain felt by the victims' families and loved ones. Along with the sorrow we felt, I think we also shared a feeling of anger toward the cowardice of the act and the desire to do anything we can to help.

Many of us were on the Las Vegas strip to attend the G2E Conference, as were many, many people in the Indian gaming and global gaming communities. We immediately reached out to our partners to offer logistical support. I, myself, just returned from Las Vegas and many of my teammates are still there.

When I was originally drafting this testimony, I was prepared to talk about the NIGC's proactive approach to regulation, about how we strive to not wait for potential problems to become crises but instead, look for areas of opportunity that allow us, within our statutory authorities, to leverage our relationships to bolster public safety and protect tribal interests.

I planned on discussing how the strong regulatory footing and sophisticated security infrastructure of Indian gaming present excellent opportunities to proactively attack safety and security risks, even where such risks are not unique to or especially prevalent in Indian Country.

Among the areas of opportunity we have identified, I planned to discuss our anti-human trafficking efforts under the leadership of our Vice Chair, Kathryn Isom-Clause, our IT vulnerability assessments created under the leadership of our technology director, Travis Waldo, that mitigate cyber security threats, and our active shooter training which, under the leadership of our training manager, Steve Brewer, represents an excellent partnership between the NIGC and DHS.

However, in light of recent horrific events in Las Vegas, our efforts feel less a success and more a mere drop in the ocean of what needs to be done. That said, narrow as our Indian gaming lane may be, the NIGC, as do all agencies, can and must focus on what we can and must do to make all of us safer within our respective missions.

This is our regulatory philosophy: proactive performance of our regulatory duties without unnecessarily inhibiting the entrepreneurial spirit of tribes. Details of our agency activity, our commitment to tribal consultation and our core initiatives are outlined in my written testimony.

As today's hearing is on issues and opportunities for the future, however, I think it is appropriate to reflect upon lessons learned since the Cabazon decision, and indeed, lessons learned from the history of Federal Indian policy. As regulators of the Indian gaming industry, the NIGC is uniquely situated to share our observations gleaned over the last 30 years. In that vein, let me discuss some 30,000 foot points.

Special care must be taken to ensure any future legislation or regulation related to IGRA that impacts gaming such as those related to taking land into trust or those that alter Federal responsibilities to tribes builds on the success of Indian gaming and provides ample flexibility for tribes to continue to strengthen their governments, including through the rebuilding of economically viable land bases.

As a general matter, I stress that we must be mindful of unintended consequences. Rather than evaluate any proposed revision or potential improvement to IGRA in a vacuum, I would encourage the Committee to test each idea against the backdrop of foundational principles of longstanding Federal Indian policy.

These foundational principles include: sound Federal policies of tribal self determination; respect for inherent tribal sovereignty; the adherence to and upholding of Federal trust responsibilities flowing from the United States' special relationship with tribal Nations and the flexibility of land policy to account for the diverse histories and land bases of the 567 federally-recognized tribes.

No one-size-fits-all approach will work in the pursuit of tribal economic development, self sufficiency and strong tribal governments—principal goals of Federal policy that IGRA explicitly and wisely recognizes.

Looking to the future, IGRA's purpose remains as relevant as ever. As regulators of Indian gaming, we recognize the overall success of Indian gaming, both in terms of regulation and economic impact. We also recognize that success is due, in large part, to IGRA's acknowledgement of tribes as primary regulators and primary beneficiaries of their operations and the previously mentioned foundational principles.

We believe an adherence to these principles as good policy and must be central in any forward looking discussions. We also note that Indian Country has uniformly made clear that the issues caused by the Seminole decision must be addressed before any amendments to IGRA are considered.

As Chairman, I stand ready to make available the expertise of the NIGC to weigh in on any IGRA-related matters. I appreciate dialogue on what improvements, if any, should be considered to strengthen the legal framework within which Indian gaming operates.

Thank you for the opportunity to address this Committee. I am happy to answer any questions you may have.

[The prepared statement of Mr. Chaudhuri follows:]

PREPARED STATEMENT OF HON. JONODEV OSCEOLA CHAUDHURI, CHAIRMAN, NATIONAL INDIAN GAMING COMMISSION

I. Introduction

Thank you Chairman Hoeven, Vice Chairman Udall, and members of the Committee for inviting me to testify today. It is an honor to appear before you as Chairman of the National Indian Gaming Commission.

Today I will provide an overview of the evolution of Indian gaming; the current state of the industry and our responsive initiatives; as well as some thoughts on the future of Indian gaming.

II. Evolution of Indian Gaming

Tribal gaming, as we think of it today, dates back to the 1970s when a number of Indian tribes established bingo operations as a means of raising revenue to fund tribal government operations and realize the goals of tribal self-determination.

The *California vs. Cabazon Band of Mission Indians* decision affirmed a tribe's right to regulate gaming on tribal lands. In that case, the United States Supreme Court recognized that a tribe may engage in gaming if it is located within a state that permits such gaming for any purpose by any person, organization, or entity. The Court also found the tribal and federal interests supporting gambling—tribal self-determination and economic self-sufficiency—preempted the state interest in regulating gaming. The Court emphasized the compelling need in Indian Country for economic development and that the gaming operations were a major source of employment.

Soon after the *Cabazon* decision, Congress took up the issue of tribal gaming and conducted a series of hearings, ultimately culminating in the passage of the Indian Gaming Regulatory Act of 1988. In addition to providing a statutory basis for gaming on Indian lands, the Act incorporates the very same reasons the Court identified in *Cabazon* as compelling: to promote economic development, self-sufficiency, and strong tribal governments. The tribes' role as primary regulators and primary beneficiaries, as well as their sovereign right to pursue gaming on their lands, was left intact, with general regulatory oversight at the federal level to be provided by the newly created National Indian Gaming Commission.

The NIGC has several specific responsibilities that it carries out pursuant to IGRA, including approving tribal gaming ordinances and management contracts with third parties and reviewing tribal gaming license decisions. We are funded entirely by fees paid by tribal gaming operations, and the current fee rate is at its lowest adopted amount since 2010. Our regulatory role is carried out at the NIGC's headquarters, located in Washington, D.C., and our seven regional offices located in: Portland, OR; Sacramento; Phoenix; St. Paul; Tulsa; Oklahoma City; and Washington, D.C. The NIGC's region offices house NIGC staff in the Compliance Division, making it possible to develop a strong working relationship with tribal gaming authorities, be accessible, and have regular contact with tribes at their gaming locations.

The NIGC is committed to fulfilling its tribal consultation obligations by adhering to the consultation framework described in the Tribal Consultation Policy. The Commission has committed to consulting with tribes before taking any action that may have a substantial direct effect on an Indian tribe on matters including, but not limited to, the ability of an Indian tribe to regulate its Indian gaming, an Indian tribe's formal relationship with the Commission, or the consideration of the Commission's trust responsibilities to Indian tribes. In fact, the Commission just completed a series of five consultations on a variety of matters, and will be engaging in another consultation at the end of October.

III. State of the Industry

Indian gaming is conducted in 28 states by 246 of the 567 federally recognized tribes. When the NIGC began tracking industry-wide gross gaming revenues in 1997, Indian gaming generated approximately $7.4 billion. In the years since, the industry has grown tremendously, with gross revenues for fiscal year 2016 reaching $31.2 billion. Gross revenue, though, does not include the costs of running a casino, including debt service. In other words, 31.2 billion, while an impressive number, does not equate to revenues making it to tribes. And, although one of the purposes of IGRA is to promote tribal self-sufficiency, gaming revenues do not supplant other federal programs, services, and obligations, but rather allow tribes to generate jobs and revenue which enable tribal governments to provide fundamental services to their communities. Many tribes have used gaming profits to fund education, improve health and elder care, enhance police and fire departments, build houses and roads, develop environmental programs, launch commercial ventures, and buy lands.

A. Success

The NIGC takes seriously its role in safeguarding the integrity of Indian gaming. Through IGRA, Indian gaming continues to support tribal economic development, self-sufficiency, and strong tribal governments. Indian gaming has an undeniable impact on Indian Country programs, services, and infrastructure affecting the lives of millions of Native peoples and citizens of local communities. Across the board, Indian gaming has infused tribal program budgets with crucial funding and has allowed tribes to provide vital services to their members.

1. Economic and Community Impact

Small and medium tribal gaming operations (those earning less than $25 million in gross gaming revenues) drive much of the industry, making up 57 percent of all gaming operations. Indian gaming has been a lifeline for these communities, supplementing funding the federal government provides. And, although tribal gaming varies in size and revenue, even the smallest gaming operations derive benefits from the industry, including much needed jobs for tribal and local community members. Gaming has also served as a catalyst for tribes to diversify their economic portfolios and has led to success in industries that were initially not available to them. Through these economic successes, tribes have been able to direct funding to other important tribal priorities such as healthcare, education, and infrastructure.

Tribes have always been the architects of their own success in the industry. As expertise and experience have developed, more and more tribes are looking beyond their own facilities to the tribal gaming landscape as a whole. The Indian gaming industry has provided a powerful platform for tribes to share their expansive knowledge, enhancing inter-tribal relations and further bolstering the well-being of Indian Country at large.

Indian gaming has an undeniably positive impact on local and state economies. It provides opportunities in some of the most economically depressed areas in the country. Indian gaming allows tribes to create and support thousands of direct and indirect jobs, to make charitable contributions, and to support local emergency services, truly impacting many lives. Its role in Indian Country as well as in surrounding communities cannot be overstated.

2. Regulatory Framework

IGRA's framework—with tribes as the primary regulators—works. Tribes themselves have the greatest interest in protecting their resources and their communities. It is a testament to the leadership of tribal governments, the regulators, and the work of their dedicated employees that the Indian gaming industry has continued to maintain security and stability. NIGC support includes working with tribal governments and their employees to ensure they have the tools necessary to protect their assets and the integrity of the industry through diligent, professional oversight and enforcement.

The NIGC remains strongly committed to upholding the statutory authority and responsibilities outlined in IGRA. We carry out these responsibilities through a comprehensive compliance approach and do not take lightly the crippling effects that closure of a casino could have on a tribe and the surrounding communities. Before the Chair takes an enforcement action, we work with tribes and our regulatory partners to address areas of concern using a variety of tools outlined in the visual below. It is worth noting that the majority of tribes achieve compliance voluntarily. This is reflective of the good work and sound partnerships the NIGC has with tribes and regulators on the ground.

We approach our regulatory role through a multi-faceted comprehensive compliance approach of technical assistance, training, and enforcement. And, with the assistance of Indian Country through consultation, we focus on regularly improving the effectiveness of our regulations. Fiscal Year 2016 has proven to be a robust year of engagement with Indian country.

Below is a list highlighting some of our fiscal year 2016 regulatory activities:

- 599 Site Visits
- 474 audit statement reviews
- 226,857 FBI fingerprint and name checks
- 185 Surveillance Reviews
- 314 Tribal Licensing issuance reviews
- 6 Internal Control Assessments (ICA)
- 2 Internal Audit Reviews
- 33 trainings events to 1,662 participants
- 18 IT Vulnerability Assessments (ITVA)

3. NIGC Initiatives

The NIGC stresses strong partnerships and consistent communication with tribal gaming operations to achieve compliance with IGRA. The Commission works with tribes to ensure they have the tools necessary to effectively regulate their operations and meet IGRA's requirements. With its statutory mission in mind, the NIGC has focused on four initiatives, which comprise the Agency's strategic plan.

Through our initiatives, we have been able to protect the integrity of Indian gaming, expand outreach, and develop new services that support gaming operations and its staff.

Protecting against anything that amounts to gamesmanship on the backs of tribes

The Commission is committed to preventing non-tribal government interests from manipulating relationships to benefit themselves to the detriment of tribal gaming operations. Ensuring tribes are the primary beneficiaries of their gaming activities lies within the core mission of the NIGC, and preventing "gamesmanship" underpins all of the Agency's activities. A recent example of protecting against gamesmanship is outlined in a settlement agreement I entered into with the Cheyenne and Arapaho Tribes of Oklahoma on April 11, 2017. After identifying, self-reporting, and providing documentation of potential gamesmanship involving a casino parking lot to the NIGC, the Tribes and NIGC entered into a settlement agreement acknowledging that there was sufficient evidence to support an enforcement action for misuse of gaming revenue and violation of the sole proprietary interest requirement.

Staying ahead of the technology curve

The Commission created its first technology division which has spearheaded numerous projects, including providing technical assistance to tribes to better evaluate and manage their security and technological vulnerabilities. As part of this initiative, the NIGC offers no-cost IT vulnerability assessments (ITVAs) for tribes and tribal regulators, which provide a tribal gaming facility with a vulnerability analysis of its IT system. An ITVA is a high level tool that assists a tribe's IT security posture relative to its gaming systems and provides a solid base-line for internal mitigation of any risk found and assists in justifying funding for third-party assistance. In fiscal year 2017, the NIGC has conducted 19 ITVAs.

IT vulnerability assessment testing consists of two types of tests: external and internal. The external test provides an overview of security vulnerabilities, which are visible from outside the gaming system network. The scan takes into account all security layers on the network between the scanner machine and the target system. The internal network test provides an overview of vulnerabilities, which are visible from the local network, taking into account host-based security controls on the target system.

The technology division is also leading the Commission's consideration of regulatory updates to better address mobile gaming devices. Mobile gaming devices are handheld electronic devices that allow casino patrons to play anywhere within the casino or potentially other locations within a tribe's gaming eligible lands, such as restaurants and hotels.

Developing effective rural outreach to smaller gaming establishments in rural areas

The focus of the Commission's Rural Outreach Initiative is to develop an effective and responsive program to support tribes with small, rural gaming operations whose needs are unique from larger tribal gaming operations near cities. Regional staff manages the initiative and engages in direct outreach. Budget and staff constraints can make attending training away from the workplace difficult. Due to this, the Commission has added virtual training sessions to its Regional Training Courses to benefit rural gaming operations that cannot always attend in person. Through the initiative, the NIGC is increasing its communications and enhancing its regulatory partnerships with tribes with small rural gaming operations.

Supporting a strong workforce both within NIGC and among regulatory partners

The Commission has enhanced regional trainings to include more hands-on learning and is leveraging technology to receive feedback. The NIGC training program seeks to improve the content and style of its training courses and is currently revising all of its training materials. For 2017, the NIGC training program has developed a two-day workshop for internal audit and internal controls development. Additionally, the NIGC has developed training to assist tribes in recognizing "gamesmanship". The NIGC's new classes are designed to provide "how-to," hands-on learning with real-life scenarios, exercises and examples, and shared best practices. Ideally, tribal leadership, tribal regulators, and operators will not only better understand the regulations but will have the tools necessary to effectively measure and maintain compliance in their operations.

The agency also recognized that due to operational demands and staffing size, attending Regional training courses may be difficult for some tribes. In fiscal year 2017, virtual training was introduced, allowing participants to register for select courses broadcast live from the regional training location. This interactive approach allows participants to ask presenters questions and actively engage in group discussions and breakouts. The NIGC is also in the early stages of rolling out a learning management system, which will provide on-line training courses and webinar-type training to tribal leadership, gaming commissioners, regulators, and operators. In 2016, the NIGC instituted knowledge reviews in certain audit related classes. The knowledge reviews seek to test the participant on how well they have learned the material and assist the NIGC in determining the efficacy of its training. The testing is done after the class is completed, and then repeated ninety days later.

4. Regulatory Review

As part of any regulatory agencies' obligation to maintain the effectiveness of its regulations, the Commission is contemplating changes to its regulations.

Draft Guidance on the Class III Minimum Internal Control Standards

The NIGC's Class III Minimum Internal Controls Standards (MICS) were promulgated in 1999 and last substantively revised in 2005. In 2006, the D.C. Circuit Court of Appeals held that NIGC lacked authority to enforce or promulgate these regulations. Since that time, the Class III MICS have remained unaltered in the federal register, but not enforced by the Agency. Technology has advanced rapidly, making some standards obsolete and introducing new areas of risk not contemplated by the outdated standards. In addition, tribal-state compacts—even those entered into since 2006—continue to adopt NIGC Class III MICS by reference. Recognizing the industry's need for updated standards, and after consultation with tribes, the Commission is developing updated, non-binding guidance for Class III MICS and a proposed rule that will address the outdated standards still remaining in the regulations.

Management Contract Regulations and Procedures

Pursuant to IGRA, Indian tribes may enter into management contracts for the operation and management of their gaming activity subject to the approval of the NIGC Chair. The Agency's regulations govern the review and approval of management contracts, including background investigations of entities and individuals with an interest in the management contract. These regulations are intended to protect the integrity of the Indian gaming industry and ensure that the tribe is the primary beneficiary of its gaming operation. The Commission recently consulted with tribes and sought industry feedback on any recommended changes to our regulations and procedures that may improve the NIGC's efficiency in processing management agreements and background investigations. Comments are being reviewed to determine next steps.

As part of its review of the management contract process, the Commission recently streamlined its National Environmental Policy Act (NEPA) process by creating a Categorical Exclusion for management contracts that do not include new construction. With the categorical exclusion in place, most contracts to manage existing facilities and most contract renewals will not be required to go through the time consuming and expensive process of obtaining an Environmental Assessment or Environmental Impact Statement. The Agency recognizes and supports the important environmental protections that NEPA provides. However, in the case of most management contracts, there simply are no environmental implications that are brought to bear by a new person or company taking over the day-to-day management of a casino. And, where construction is part of the agreement, the categorical exclusion will not be applied and the NEPA process will proceed as normal.

Fees

The Commission is considering amending the language of our fee regulations to improve the fee rate analysis and to allow publication of the fee rate to coincide with the completion of our budget for the fiscal year and the annual release of the industry's Gross Gaming Revenue. Additionally, we anticipate this amendment would reduce the margin of error for fee calculations as the rate would be set only once within a fiscal year.

25 C.F.R. Part 547 Class II Gaming Systems

The NIGC initially implemented Technical Standards in 2008 requiring that before a Class II gaming system may be placed on the floor and offered to the public for play, it must be submitted to an independent gaming laboratory which would test the system against the Technical Standards.

It was recognized by tribes, the industry, and NIGC that implementation of the Technical Standards would come at a financial cost to tribes. Of particular concern however, was the potential financial burden on bringing gaming systems that had already been manufactured and/or put into play—and "compliant" with applicable law in the absence of the Technical Standards—into compliance with the new 2008 rule. Thus, to reduce that cost, the NIGC provided that gaming systems manufactured prior to issuance of the standards in 2008 could be certified to an alternate minimum standard, but made fully compliant or removed from the gaming floor within five years. In 2012, that "sunset provision" was extended another five years, to November 10, 2018. After extensive internal review of the technical standards and consultation with the industry, the Commission determined that it was appropriate to remove this deadline, provided that such systems are subject to additional annual review by tribal gaming regulators and with certain records and information regarding that review to be made available to the NIGC. The Commission carefully considered comments received on the issue and published a Notice of Proposed Rulemaking in the Federal Register on September 28, 2017.

5. Developing Partnerships to Stamp Out Human Trafficking

The NIGC had forged partnerships to enhance its proactive regulatory approach to educate and provide resources to combat human trafficking. While the NIGC is not aware of any data suggesting human trafficking is any more rampant in Indian gaming than any other large commercial activity with heavy customer movement, we recognize the industry's strong regulatory structure that provides the agency an area of opportunity to support broader efforts to stamp out human trafficking. Beginning in January 2017, the Agency's forward-looking approach allowed the Commission to partner with the Bureau of Indian Affairs, the Department of Homeland Security, the Department of Justice, the National Human Trafficking Hotline and other federal and non-profit organizations to provide engagement, tools and resources at our regional training conferences.

B. Challenges

While Indian gaming continues to be successful, it is not without its challenges. To that end, NIGC receives input from tribes and stakeholders through consultation efforts, daily interactions, site visits, and by observing the work of other agencies supporting Indian Country.

As we see the tremendous growth of the Indian gaming industry, it is more important than ever to not lose sight of the policies underlying IGRA. Indian gaming, while potentially lucrative, is a governmental activity, not a mere commercial enterprise. This simple idea is sometimes forgotten, but crucial when discussing Indian gaming. IGRA requires that gaming revenues are owned by, and benefit, the entire tribe rather than any particular individual; tribes may only use net revenues from their IGRA gaming for five limited governmental purposes.

Related to the misperception that IGRA gaming is a commercial, rather than a governmental, endeavor is the notion that gaming on Indian lands not within the narrow limitations of reservation boundaries is somehow inconsistent with IGRA. The narrative of "off-reservation gaming" has the potential to distract from the underlying principle behind Indian gaming—that Indian gaming development is an expression of a tribe's sovereignty and desire to provide governmental services to its people. Gaming on Indian lands, which can include reservation, trust, and restricted fee land, is what IGRA contemplates. That being said, the NIGC understands concerns may arise when a tribe decides to open a casino on a particular parcel of land. As a regulatory agency, however, our role is limited to ensuring gaming takes place on eligible Indian lands. And, although the definition of Indian lands includes reservation land, it also includes non-reservation trust and restricted fee lands over which the tribe exercises governmental power. While IGRA also prohibits gaming on trust lands acquired by tribes after 1988, it does provide for measured flexibility allowing for gaming on eligible Indian lands, besides reservation lands, in clear recognition of the diversity of histories and land bases in Indian country. This flexibility supports the goals of tribal economic development and strong tribal governments (through the rebuilding of land bases) and is consistent with the principal goals set forth in its findings.

IV. Thoughts on the Future

IGRA's purpose remains as relevant as ever for the future of Indian gaming, with its inevitable technological evolution and expansion. The policies of IGRA have provided tribes with the support, guidance, and protection to develop a healthy, robust gaming industry. The NIGC will continue to adapt to industry advancements and work to ensure a well-regulated gaming industry that supports tribal economic development, tribal self-sufficiency, and strong tribal governments. The NIGC is unique in its expertise and great working relationships with tribal regulators and operations. Any new technology or advancement in gaming such as i-gaming, fantasy sports, or mobile gaming will have a learning curve, but the NIGC's knowledgeable and dedicated staff is up to the task of addressing those issues without undermining the intent of IGRA.

The success of the Indian gaming industry is due in large part to the expertise tribes have developed in running and regulating their operations. The Commission believes any potential legislation related to gaming must include tribes and provide a level playing field of opportunity for Indian country. Potential legislation addressing new gaming markets, such as Internet gaming or the increased availability of sports betting, etc., must include dialogue with State, industry, and other stakeholders in considering regulatory structures for emerging markets and IGRA's foundational principle of supporting tribal economic development, self-sufficiency, and strong tribal governments must be the primary guide. The federal government's special relationship with tribes is a bedrock of federal law and policy. IGRA's tribal self-determination principles have resulted in the integrity and economic success of

Indian gaming thus far, and should inform future dialogue regarding national gaming policy. Congress can ensure that the benefits of Indian gaming are preserved and not lost in an on-line environment in which a handful of first-to-market interests dominate.

Although technologic advancements and the face of gaming is very much on everyone's minds as IGRA approaches its thirtieth anniversary, we must also be mindful of other aspects of the Act. For example, we at the NIGC have repeatedly heard from Tribes that the issue created by the United States Supreme Court case, *Seminole Tribe of Florida v. Florida* must be addressed. In that case, the United States Supreme Court concluded that in IGRA, Congress did not waive States' immunity from suit by Indian Tribes. Thus, tribes are unable sue states for failing to negotiate compacts in good faith, thus shifting the balance of power in tribal-state compact negotiations to states. We agree that without a *Seminole* fix, the intended parity between Class III tribal gaming and commercial gaming may further deteriorate. And, as with any proposed legislation or new developments with Indian gaming, NIGC stands ready to work with Congress, tribes, and other stakeholders to uphold the foundational principles of IGRA.

With any changes to IGRA, though, special care must be taken to ensure any future legislation or regulation related to IGRA that impacts gaming such as those related to taking land into trust or that alter federal responsibilities to tribes, builds on the success of Indian gaming and provides ample flexibility for tribes to continue to strengthen their governments, including through the rebuilding of economically-viable land bases. As a general matter, I stress that we must be mindful of unintended consequences. Some of the most disastrous federal policies from the perspective of tribal nations were the product of the good intentions of purported advocates of Native peoples. IGRA, however, does not fall into that category. And rather than evaluate any proposed revision or potential improvement to IGRA in a vacuum, I would encourage the Committee to test each idea against a backdrop of the foundational principles of longstanding federal Indian policy.

As regulators of Indian gaming, we recognize the overall success of Indian gaming over the last 30 years, both in terms of regulation and economic impact. We also recognize that that success is due in large part to IGRA's acknowledgment of the tribes' sovereign right to pursue gaming on their lands, its preservation of their role as primary regulators and primary beneficiaries of their operations, and its protection of varied avenues to allow tribes with diverse histories, land bases, and capacities to pursue gaming. We believe an adherence to these self-determination principles and flexibility that accounts for historic realities is good policy and must be central in any forward-looking discussions. As Chairman, I stand ready to make available the expertise of the NIGC to weigh-in on any IGRA-related matters, and I appreciate dialogue on what improvements, if any, should be considered to strengthen the legal framework within which Indian gaming operates.

V. Conclusion

In the nearly 30 years since the Indian Gaming Regulatory Act was passed, the Indian gaming industry has grown, matured, and evolved in ways that almost no one could have predicted at the time. And while that growth is due primarily to the ingenuity and hard work of the tribal communities that built the industry, it has occurred in the context of a piece of legislation that was enacted with core goals in mind—to promote tribal economic development, tribal self-sufficiency, and strong tribal governments. The NIGC takes seriously its role to regulate the Indian gaming industry to ensure these goals are achieved. These efforts in conjunction with IGRA's sound principles will continue guiding Indian gaming into a bright and prosperous future.

The CHAIRMAN. Thank you.
Mr. Tahsuda.

STATEMENT OF JOHN TAHSUDA, III, PRINCIPAL DEPUTY ASSISTANT SECRETARY, INDIAN AFFAIRS, U.S. DEPARTMENT OF THE INTERIOR

Mr. TAHSUDA. Good afternoon, Chairman Hoeven, Vice Chairman Udall and members of the Committee.

My name is John Tahsuda and I am the Acting Assistant Secretary for Indian Affairs at the Department of the Interior. Thank you for the opportunity to testify before this Committee on the department's role in Indian gaming. You have my full written testimony. I will offer some more brief oral remarks.

The passage of the Indian Gaming Regulatory Act, IGRA, provided a means of promoting tribal economic development, self sufficiency and strong tribal governments through well regulated gaming. Indian gaming has resulted in considerable financial resources for a wide range of tribal services and programs from education and housing to law enforcement and health care and has bolstered jobs in local and tribal communities.

That said, the Department is mindful that while gaming has great potential to improve economic conditions for tribal and non-tribal communities, it could also introduce new complications to communities, including drain on local resources, increased traffic, visitation and crime, such as drugs and prostitution.

The Department, under Secretary Zinke's leadership, firmly believes there needs to be thoughtful and thorough consideration of all factors relating to gaming applications. Given our commitment to being a good neighbor and steward, we believe local voices must have a fair opportunity to provide insight and input into these decisions.

That is why an in-depth and balanced consideration of all factors will be at the core of the department's decision-making process for any off-reservation gaming or land-into-trust applications. We will closely adhere to the law when reviewing tribal gaming matters as detailed in IGRA, but also plan to put more emphasis on all of the applicable criteria.

No single criteria by itself will be considered dispositive in these intricate proposals. Nor will local communities be denied an opportunity to voice their concerns. We are committed to striking a balance between differing interests which we fully recognize are prevalent in these matters while following the provisions of the law.

In addition to being more thoughtful when considering gaming and fee-to-trust proposals, Interior is also committed to providing tribes realistic expectations during the formal review process. For instance, in the case of off-reservation land into trust efforts, the commitment of time and resources required can be exorbitant, particularly if that proposal is denied.

Therefore, we believe it is important to be upfront about proposals that may not be acceptable and, as a result, we are considering changes to our land-into-trust process to provide feedback earlier in the process.

The Department does recognize that equities may be different for restored and landless tribes when it comes to off-reservation gaming and land-into-trust proposals. Interior is committed to reviewing all the factors and seeking broad input in its decision-making process for these applications.

In conclusion, the Department is committed to being thorough and balanced in our considerations for both trust land acquisitions and gaming proposals. We will closely adhere to the law when reviewing these matters, putting emphasis on all the applicable criteria and ensuring that local communities will not be denied an opportunity to voice concerns.

I, along with our team at Interior, welcome the opportunity to work with this Committee and Congress on Indian gaming matters, recognizing the plenary authority Congress holds in all tribal matters.

Thank you for the opportunity to testify today. I am pleased to answer any questions you may have.

[The prepared statement of Mr. Tahsuda follows:]

PREPARED STATEMENT OF JOHN TAHSUDA, III, PRINCIPAL DEPUTY ASSISTANT SECRETARY, INDIAN AFFAIRS, U.S. DEPARTMENT OF THE INTERIOR

Good afternoon Chairman Hoeven, Vice Chairman Udall, and Members of the Committee. My name is John Tahsuda and I am the Acting Assistant Secretary for Indian Affairs at the Department of the Interior (Department or Interior). Thank you for the opportunity to testify before this Committee on the Department's role in Indian gaming.

The framework for Indian gaming both on and off reservation was established by Congress with the passage of the Indian Gaming Regulatory Act (IGRA) [Pub.L. 100–497, 25 U.S.C. § 2701 et seq.] in 1988. The regulatory scheme codified into law assigns the Department certain responsibilities for regulating gaming on Indian lands. As laid out in IGRA, Class I gaming is regulated exclusively by Indian tribal governments; Class II gaming regulation is reserved to tribal governments in cooperation with the Federal Government; and, Class III gaming is regulated primarily by tribal governments in cooperation with the federal government and, to the extent negotiated in an approved compact, a state government. Under IGRA, Interior reviews and determines whether to approve tribal-state gaming compacts and fee-to-trust applications for gaming.

The passage of IGRA serves as recognition on behalf of Congress that well-regulated gaming provided a means of promoting tribal economic development, self-sufficiency, and strong tribal governments. Indian gaming has resulted in considerable financial resources for a wide range of tribal services and programs, from education and housing to law enforcement and health care, and has bolstered jobs in local and tribal communities.

That said, the Department is mindful that, while gaming has great potential to improve economic conditions for tribal and non-tribal communities, it can also introduce new complications to communities, including a drain on local resources, increased traffic, visitation, and crime, such as drugs and prostitution. The Department, under Secretary Zinke's leadership, firmly believes there needs to be a thoughtful and thorough consideration of all factors relating to gaming applications. Given our commitment to being a good neighbor and steward, we believe local voices must have a fair opportunity to provide insight and input into these decisions.

This emphasis on a balanced process is also critical for the acquisition of trust lands located off reservation, which the Department firmly believes should move forward in tandem with federal consideration of tribal gaming. The Department previously testified during the 115th Congress about its role in the fee-to-trust process, which can be further complicated by the prospect of off reservation gaming. Off-reservation lands that are acquired through the Fee-to-Trust process have the potential to raise jurisdictional uncertainties in local communities, as well as complicating land-use planning and the provision of services. Moreover, non-Indian communities may experience tax revenue consequences if payments in lieu of taxes are not agreed upon. Ultimately, the Department has received comments that taking land located off reservation into trust for gaming can introduce economic or other conditions that can have significant impacts on the immediate and surrounding communities. As a result, the Department's off-reservation trust regulations require particular attention to issues of jurisdiction and taxation.

Off-reservation trust acquisitions also raise the possibility that a tribe may initiate gaming operations once the land is held in trust by the federal government, even though that was not in the original plan. This matter continues to complicate and isolate some communities near these facilities. In those instances, local communities that may have offered support or participated in the process could now need to engage in a new public input process.

Collectively, this is why an in-depth and balanced consideration of all factors will be at the core of the Department's decisionmaking process for any off reservation gaming or land into trust applications. The Department will closely adhere to the law when reviewing tribal gaming matters as detailed in IGRA, but also plans to put more emphasis on all of the applicable criteria. No single criteria by itself will be considered dispositive in these intricate proposals, nor will local communities be denied an opportunity to voice their concerns. We are committed to striking a balance between differing interests, which we fully recognize are prevalent in these matters, while following the provisions of the law.

In addition to being more thoughtful when considering gaming and fee-to-trust proposals, Interior is also committed to providing tribes realistic expectations during the formal review process. For instance, in the case of off reservation land into trust efforts, the commitment of time and resources required can be exorbitant, particularly if that proposal is denied. Therefore, we believe it is important to be upfront about proposals that may not be acceptable. As a result, we are considering changes to our land-into-trust process [25 CFR § 151] to provide feedback earlier in the process.

The Department recognizes that the equities may be different for restored tribes and landless tribes when it comes to off reservation gaming and land into trust proposals. For example, the Department is currently reviewing the Shawnee Tribe of Oklahoma's fee-to-trust. The Shawnee are a landless tribe and, given the unavailability of land in close proximity to its members, the Tribe elected to explore other alternatives. They have worked closely in collaboration with other Oklahoma tribes, the Governor of Oklahoma, the local community, and a number of Members of the Congressional delegation to identify and secure a potential location. While a decision on that acquisition is pending with the Department, Interior is committed to reviewing all factors and seeking broad input in its decision making.

As this Committee looks ahead at the next thirty years of Indian gaming, the Department sees an opportunity to think strategically about its own role. Our commitment is to be thorough and balanced in our considerations for both trust land acquisitions and gaming proposals. The Department will closely adhere to the law when reviewing these matters, putting emphasis on all the applicable criteria and ensuring that local communities will not be denied an opportunity to voice concerns. The Department welcomes the opportunity to work with this Committee and the Congress on Indian gaming matters, recognizing the plenary authority Congress holds in all tribal matters. If there is interest in further discussing these issues, we stand ready and able to work with you.

This concludes my written statement. Thank you for the opportunity to testify today and I am pleased to answer any questions you may have.

The CHAIRMAN. Thank you to you both.

I am going to begin with Chairman Chaudhuri.

In 2015, this Committee held an oversight hearing to receive testimony on the GAO report, Indian Gaming, Regulation and Oversight by the Federal Government, States and Tribes. More recently, the GAO confirmed that as of December 2016, the NIGC has yet to comply with all of their recommendations outlined in that report.

Would you please give us an update, Chairman, as to where you are with the GAO recommendations from that report?

Mr. CHAUDHURI. Thank you, Chairman.

As we mentioned at that time, we absolutely welcomed GAO's inquiry. We also welcomed their ongoing work with us to identify areas of opportunity for us to improve our services.

We were actually ahead of GAO in some of the recommendations regarding some of the knowledge reviews that we are in the process of implementing to tie our trainings to actual efficacy of our regulatory approach. Those knowledge reviews, frankly, came from discussions between our staff and members of the Committee.

I am actually thankful for some of the work that collectively we are doing together to make sure we are having the most efficient trainings possible.

The GAO mentioned a few areas of opportunity. One in particular was working to have deadlines attached when we tried to provide technical assistance to tribes identified as having compliance issues. Since the GAO report, we have put firm deadlines into each and every letter of concern and awareness that we provided to our regulatory partners.

We have also instituted metrics tracking with our trainings. That again flows from the GAO report and our discussions with the Committee.

Finally, we are actively involved in measuring our ability to provide resources to facilities with some of the most challenging capacity issues. Those all relate to the GAO's recommendations.

As a final note, outreach was part of GAO's report. I am pleased to say in our last attempt to provide clarity to the industry involving trying to develop non-binding Class III mix in light of the CRIT decision, we have made special efforts to reach out to our State partners to loop them in on our draft language.

We are sensitive to GAO's findings, but I do want to say the overall thrust of GAO's report was that the industry overall was healthy and the regulatory structure overall was strong. There were, of course, recommendations, as there are with any report, but we very much appreciated the overall thrust of the report.

The CHAIRMAN. You do not anticipate any problem meeting the recommendations they made in the report?

Mr. CHAUDHURI. None whatsoever.

The CHAIRMAN. Thank you.

Last month, the Securities and Exchange Commission acknowledged that it had been hacked. Under the previous Administration, the Office of Personnel Management, as you will recall, exposed millions of Federal employees' personal information to cyber criminals.

My question is, what is the Commission doing to ensure that the critical information tribes report to you is secure and have you been subject to any type of software or cyber security breaches?

Mr. CHAUDHURI. Thank you Chairman, cyber security is a concern for the gaming industry as it is for all industries and governmental agencies. This is the age we live in. There is one report that said if you leave an unsecured device exposed to the Internet, you are guaranteed not just dozens, not just hundreds, but potentially thousands of attacks in a short amount of time if you do not have sufficient firewalls and safety measures in place. This is the reality of the arena in which we live.

Recognizing that and recognizing our role as supporting our regulatory partners, each tribe having its own regulatory body, we have looked at our internal capabilities to figure out where we can be of the most help. Through our recently created technology division to stay ahead of the technology curve, I think we developed a pretty innovative approach to this challenge.

We developed what are called IT vulnerability assessments by which we will go to any tribe that requests it and perform a 360 review of cyber vulnerabilities for that tribe. This is a relatively new program but since starting, I have some numbers here that are pretty good.

Since starting, this is a year and a half old, the program has hit the ball out of the park and 19 ITVAs were performed this year alone. There is a waiting list now, not a long waiting list but it has been very well received in Indian Country.

We need to distinguish between cyber vulnerabilities and cyber compromises. Cyber attacks are always ongoing. I mentioned the idea about an unprotected system. All the time there are cyber attacks.

In terms of cyber compromises, fortunately because of the work of tribal regulators with supportive agencies such as ours, examples of actual cyber compromises are relatively few and far between.

The CHAIRMAN. That is encouraging to hear.

I am going to a little bit more time hoping to get this done in one round. I will provide the same courtesy to my fellow Senators. I think that might save having to have two rounds because we do have a vote at 3:15 p.m.

For Secretary Tahsuda, the Indian Gaming Regulatory Act is a delicate balance between Federal, State and tribal interests. Your written testimony indicated that evaluating off-reservation gaming and land into trust, in doing so, the department was "committed to striking a balance between differing interests which we fully recognize are prevalent in these matters while following the provisions of the law."

Can you explain how you intend to strike that balance in terms of your application for these compacts?

Mr. TAHSUDA. When we say considering all the factors, I think that includes both if there is a compact under consideration as well as land and the consideration of factors there and in consideration of the factors under the land decision as well.

Some of those overlap but we believe that in the past, there have been times when greater consideration has been given to one set of factors over others. Our commitment is to weigh all the relevant factors and come to a fair and balanced conclusion based on the totality of the factors.

The CHAIRMAN. Do you intend to utilize a commutability standard for off-reservation acquisitions for gaming?

Mr. TAHSUDA. When it comes to land into trust, we are required by our regulations to consider the distance from the reservation for off-reservation applications. We also are required by IGRA to consider the positive impacts to the tribe if there is going to be gaming on that land which we believe must mean something more than mere financial gain. Things like employment opportunities, ability to host cultural activities, and community activities in the facility should all be part of the considerations impacted by the distance from the reservation.

The CHAIRMAN. Thank you.

Vice Chairman Udall.

Senator UDALL. Thank you, Mr. Chairman.

IGRA's goals of promoting tribal economic development, tribal self sufficiency and a strong tribal government are rooted in the recognition of formal government-to-government relations between the Federal Government and the tribes, as both of you know.

Every President since Nixon has embraced those goals. President Clinton specifically recognized the Federal Government's responsibility to coordinate and consult with tribal governments by issuing Executive Order 13175. President Bush issued a memorandum supporting that Executive Order as did President Obama.

For Assistant Secretary Tahsuda, will President Trump issue any Executive Memorandum or Guidance that continues the important commitments contained in Executive Order 13175?

Mr. TAHSUDA. I cannot answer that question. I think that is in the President's prerogative. What I do know is that he and Secretary Zinke have impressed upon us that we are to be guided by respect for tribal sovereignty. We have in place our consultation policies and we closely follow those and fully intend to do that through the future.

Senator UDALL. Can I have your commitment that you, as the highest ranking political appointee in Indian Affairs at Interior, that you will ensure meaningful tribal consultations occur in the spirit of that Executive Order?

Mr. TAHSUDA. Yes. Our goal is to have effective consultation with the tribes so that we can provide better outcomes as we perform our services to the tribes.

Senator UDALL. We would like it in writing at any point if you decide to issue an Executive Order on that and be notified of that.

Mr. TAHSUDA. Certainly, Senator.

Senator UDALL. Thank you.

I was hoping both of you would shed some light on IGRA's intent regarding parity between tribes and States in negotiating compacts. Do you think that balance is tipping in any way that the law did not intend?

Mr. CHAUDHURI. Thank you, Vice Chairman.

In terms of the balance and thorough approach, I would say a couple things. First of all, IGRA is specifically intended to benefit Indian tribes for the Federal policy purposes set forth in IGRA of strong tribal governments, self sufficiency, and economic development. It is legislation specifically intended to benefit tribes.

Furthermore, in terms of considering balancing considerations, there is a long recognized special relationship between the Federal Government and tribal nations as recognized in the long history of Federal case law, as well as the congressional record.

Prior to IGRA, the Cabazon decision acknowledged the tribes' inherent authority to regulate their own gaming activities. IGRA, in many ways, can only be described as an infringement on the inherent authority of tribes to regulate their own activities. It was an infringement that brought with it a very special balancing of various interests, State interests and tribal interests but it protected tribal sovereignty to ensure that if that balance was ever tilted too far in one direction, for instance, where a State were not to negotiate in good faith with a tribe, a tribe would have recourse to restore that balance. That recourse would be litigating over the State's actions and negotiations, litigating over good faith.

That balance was changed dramatically by the Seminole decision so that the carefully crafted balance of sovereign interests that IGRA sought to establish has forever since been impacted. I think Indian Country has been very clear and very thankful for today's discussion if any potential changes to IGRA are on the table, and restoring the balance that IGRA established between States and tribes needs to be the first point of discussion. Indian Country's perspective on that matter, given IGRA's intent, appears reasonable.

Senator UDALL. Mr. Secretary, your thoughts on that?

Mr. TAHSUDA. It is my understanding, I was not here at the time, but Congress is the one that sought to achieve a balance through IGRA itself. That is reflected in the statute. The statute directs us to take certain actions, to make certain reviews and consider certain criteria. We do that to the best of our ability.

It is true that the Supreme Court has its opportunity to weigh in on legislation that Congress passes and when those decisions affect longstanding practices held by our department, it does create complications for us, but it is Congress' job ultimately to simplify or clarify that if it feels the need to do that. Otherwise, it is our responsibility to apply the law the best we can.

Senator UDALL. As I mentioned in my opening, Indian gaming is an important economic engine. In New Mexico, for example the Pueblos of Santa Clara and the Ohkay Owingeh casinos employ more than 1,000 people in the Espanola Valley. The President has spoken at length about creating jobs and cutting red tape, yet Interior just released an advance notice of rulemaking that suggests Interior may revisit regulatory obstacles from the Bush years.

Mr. Assistant Secretary, in your written testimony, you state that "local voices must have a fair opportunity to provide insight and input in land-into-trust decisions." Can you elaborate and how do the current regulations fail in this regard, specifically focusing on how you believe those current regulations fail?

Mr. TAHSUDA. I did not intend, at least in my statement, to imply that our current regulations fail that. I think it is our belief that past actions by the department over the past few years did not adequately apply our regulations as they should have so that all the factors and criteria to be considered were not adequately considered. As I said earlier, some were given greater priority over others.

It is our commitment to consider all the factors we are required to consider by the law and by our regulations and apply those to the factual situation in front of us.

Senator UDALL. Interior owes Indian Country no less than to meet in and with communities that will be hardest hit by this Administration's proposed changes. What is Interior's plan to consult with tribes on the Part 151 proposal? Does it go beyond ordinary APA notice or comment such as conducting regional consultations?

Mr. TAHSUDA. It is our intent, if we move forward with changing the regulations to hold a consultation schedule. We actually should have out within the next day or so a Dear Tribal Leader letter which will identify a meeting to discuss in broad terms what we are thinking. Then we will lay out a schedule of tribal consultations in different regions around the Country. I am happy to share that with you, Mr. Vice Chairman.

Senator UDALL. Thank you very much.

The CHAIRMAN. Senator Heitkamp.

STATEMENT OF HON. HEIDI HEITKAMP, U.S. SENATOR FROM NORTH DAKOTA

Senator HEITKAMP. Thank you, Mr. Chairman.

If I could just take a minute to talk about an issue we had a hearing on last week, Mr. Chairman, I appreciate your response to the letter that I and other members of this Committee sent on human trafficking and I am glad to hear that the National Indian Gaming Commission is doing its job to educate and provide resources to combat human trafficking.

You mentioned in your testimony that your organization is not aware of any data that suggests human trafficking is more rampant in Indian gaming than other similar industries. How do you think we can collect the data so that we can be better informed and don't you think it would be valuable to have that information?

Mr. CHAUDHURI. Absolutely, and we stand ready to work with any partners to collect data as broadly as possible. As I mentioned in my oral testimony, our regulation philosophy is one of proactive regulation. While we absolutely support the gathering of data that will help target effective regulatory action, I do not think an agency needs to wait for the data to come in to recognize there are opportunities to help stamp out human trafficking as they exist.

In this regard, I really have to thank our Vice Chair, Kathryn Isom-Clause, who within the agency, has taken the leadership position to get each and every one of us on board to work with Federal partners, tribal partners, industry partners to do whatever we can.

It starts with data. We are here to work with data collection agencies that have better tools than we do as regulators but that does not mean we cannot start doing what we can now. We are doing it through our trainings and we are doing it through our participation with the Tribal Gaming Protection Network. We have the National Indian Gaming Association here and the American Gaming Association is involved with that. We are active but data is absolutely needed.

Senator HEITKAMP. We know that events and the hospitality industry are particularly targets for this kind of behavior and criminal activity. We want to make sure all of the people involved in your industry, whether it is the hotel that is attached or people on the floor watching what is going on, are well trained and can recognize the signs of human trafficking, especially when it involves small children.

Mr. Assistant Secretary, as we talk about combating drug and human trafficking and domestic violence in the context of gaming, I think it is extremely important that law enforcement has enough resources to effectively respond to these cases.

All across our region, we are seeing more and more law enforcement jails, more and more detention centers being shut down by order of various Federal agencies. That creates a real void in Indian Country in terms of access to resources, especially as it requires cooperation given jurisdictional challenges and the customers of gaming associations.

What are you doing to build more momentum for additional law enforcement resources both in terms of personnel and in terms of jail capacity?

Mr. TAHSUDA. Good question, Senator. I thought you were going to ask me something about gaming.

Senator HEITKAMP. I think this is about gaming. I think that when we are looking at the additional challenges that gaming brings to Indian Country, if you take an isolated reservation in North Dakota, you are not going to see a lot of people the tribal court would not have jurisdiction over. But once you have gambling, that hopefully is bringing more people who are going to enjoy the hospitality, but it has challenges.

There are two sides to this. I just have to tell you I think that these are issues that are associated and could, in fact, be exacerbated by Indian gaming and casino gambling in Indian Country.

Mr. TAHSUDA. Let me do my best to answer your question and ask that you bear with me. I am still pretty new in the job and trying to get a handle on everything we are doing. I still receive briefings nearly every day from our various offices and bureaus.

I do know that some of our staff came before you last week to talk about the human trafficking issue. Based on that, you probably have as good or better information than I do on that.

I do know that they are actively engaged both with sort of the industry side, with the tribal casino folks and with tribal law enforcement to try to get training for them to identify both the related drug trafficking and the human trafficking issues and to help them learn to identify situations when these may arise whether at a tribal gaming facility, tribal hospitality or any other location like a truck stop. I know that is also a big source of concern. We are actively working on that.

It is true that an activity like gaming brings a lot of people and traffic to an area that otherwise would not come there. As I referenced earlier, those are complications for the community they are required to deal with. To the extent possible, we have long been proponents of the tribes working cooperatively with local law enforcement, cross deputizing agreements to help them work through those and where appropriate, to bring Federal resources to those.

Senator HEITKAMP. I am out of time but I do want you to know that I consider the lack of law enforcement resources in Indian Country, especially for our gaming tribes, to be one of the most critical issues Indian Country is confronting.

We have longstanding, historic socioeconomic issues we need to address but if people are not safe, if people are not protected, this has to be one of your top priorities in your Acting role. We do not want to waste anymore time waiting for someone who is not Acting. I think it is critically important that law enforcement be a top priority.

Thank you, Mr. Chairman.

Mr. CHAUDHURI. Senator, if I may add one point on that. One of the master strokes of IGRA was preserving the tribes' place as the primary regulators of their gaming activity. That was important because of all people who have the strongest interest in protecting their communities, tribes have the strongest interest in protecting the health and welfare of their members as well as their patrons.

We see our work, in terms of human trafficking, as doing whatever we can to support tribal regulator efforts on the ground. Tribes are on it. I had a conversation with my good friend, Jamie Hummingbird, who heads the National Tribal Gaming Commissioners and Regulators. We spoke about this very issue.

Thank you so much for your attention to this very, very important issue.

The CHAIRMAN. I have one final question for the Chairman. I am asking this on behalf of Senator Udall who had to go vote. He had one other question for you and a follow up question.

The Tenth Circuit issued two opinions that affect the Pueblo of Pojoaque. One decision validated Part 291 which means that tribes in the Tenth Circuit can no longer look to Interior if a State decides it does not want to negotiate a compact.

The other Tenth Circuit decision now allows States to regulate vendors in a way that disrupts tribal gaming operations.

If Interior cannot issue secretarial procedures, what options do tribes have now? Does that outcome reflect IGRA's intent to put tribes and States on equal footing during the compact negotiation process?

Mr. CHAUDHURI. Thank you, Chairman, and by extension, thank you to the Vice Chair. I have two things very briefly.

The compacting analysis affects Class III gaming. Class II gaming is always within the purview of tribal communities.

The second point, it is a great question, especially given the Tenth Circuit decisions. Our role, as an agency, was to try to promote our statutory mission as best we could, given the complexities of matters on the ground with Pojoaque. In other words, we made sure that operations were safe, that assets were protected, while these matters played out.

It raises a larger question that was alluded to in the Vice Chairman's previous dialogue regarding the balance between tribal and State interests. IGRA contemplated a very delicate balance between tribes and States, one in which States would negotiate in good faith with tribes and tribes would have recourse to bring an action when that good faith did not occur.

The Seminole decision complicated that. As regulators, with an eye towards integrity and fairness, we cannot help but recognize that has created complications within the regulatory landscape. Seminole has created complications in terms of the relationship between tribes and States and it has had regulatory impacts.

In terms of how that is played out with vendors, when tribes do not have that recourse, States are free to leverage their position with tribes much more freely and are becoming more and more creative about how to leverage those positions such as bringing pressure on vendors.

The CHAIRMAN. I would like to thank both witnesses on our first panel. That will conclude our first panel and we will move to our second panel.

Thank you.

Mr. CHAUDHURI. Thank you very much, Chairman.

Mr. TAHSUDA. Thank you, Chairman.

The CHAIRMAN. We will proceed with the second panel. I would like to thank all of the witnesses.

First, we will hear from the Honorable Keeny Escalanti, President, Fort Yuma Quechan Indian Tribe, Yuma, Arizona. Then we will hear from: the Honorable Harold "Gus" Frank, Chairman, Forest County Potawatomi, Crandon, Wisconsin; the Honorable Leonard Forsman, Chairman, the Suquamish Tribe, Suquamish, Washington; and my old horseback riding partner, Ernest L. Stevens,

Jr., Chairman, National Indian Gaming Association. Thanks to all of you for being here.

Mr. Escalanti, if you will start.

STATEMENT OF HON. KEENY ESCALANTI, PRESIDENT, FORT YUMA QUECHAN INDIAN TRIBE

Mr. ESCALANTI. Good afternoon, Chairman Hoeven, Vice Chairman Udall and members of the Committee.

My name is Keeny Escalanti, Sr., President of the Quechan Indian Tribe of the Fort Yuma Indian Reservation. I thank you for the opportunity to testify today on behalf of our 3,900 members regarding benefits of gaming to our community.

According to our creation story, our people, pronounced KWAT'SAN, have lived along the Colorado River near the confluence of the Gila River. We are well known for our distinct language, the Yuman, which is a native dialect of the Hokan. Our reservation encompasses approximately 45,000 acres with a land base that is located in both California and Arizona, which shares a border with Mexico.

Our tribe is an agricultural community. We also rely on tourism and, of course, gaming to augment our economy. Our tribes operate two casinos, the Quechan Casino Resort located in Imperial County, California and Paradise Casino located in Yuma County, Arizona.

The revenues derived from these two casinos have allowed our tribe to invest in our local community and has strengthened our relationship with the local government and improved the livelihoods of our tribal and non-tribal residents.

The tribe signed our first gaming compact with the State of California in 1999 and amended it in 2006. To alleviate the financial hardship from the 2006 amendment, we recently negotiated a new compact with Governor Brown. We are grateful for the hard work of Governor Brown's Administration in this process.

The new compact recognized the benefits of investing gaming revenues in the local community and acknowledges the tribe as a significant contributor to the local economy. Under the new compact, the tribe is relieved from burdensome revenue-sharing requirements. Now the tribe can invest gaming revenues and provide important programs to its tribal membership and local residents.

Gaming has improved the well being of the tribe and the surrounding area through job creation, local investments and intergovernment collaboration, improving the safety and security of the entire community.

Gaming has created significant employment opportunities. For example, the Quechan Casino Resort in Imperial County, which has an unemployment rate of 24 percent, employs over 500 individuals. Paradise Casino in Yuma County, which has an unemployment rate of 16 percent, has over 150 employees.

In addition to job creation, gaming has allowed the tribe to create essential community and social services programs. For example, we offer scholarships and grants for post secondary education and vocational programs.

We also operate a senior citizen center that offers meals, recreation and activities of the tribe and non-Native residents.

Our tribe is especially proud of the new Ft. Yuma Health Care Center. Construction will be completed in March 2018. The new facility will be utilized jointly by the Quechan and the Cocopah Tribes. The facility will offer a clinic, dental and optical services to both tribe and non-Native residents.

Finally, gaming has fostered strong, intergovernmental relationships ensuring the safety and well being of the surrounding communities. In California, we have a strong relationship with Imperial County law enforcement and the fire prevention agency.

At the Federal level, we are one of only two tribes that has a port of entry. The Andrade Port of Entry is located on our reservation. Our Tribal Fish and Game Department and Tribal Police Department work collaboratively with the United State Border Patrol on issues of border protection and homeland security.

Looking ahead at the next 30 years, our tribe is hopeful that more States will appreciate the opportunities created through the use of gaming revenues by rural tribes.

I thank you for your time and will be happy to answer any of the Committee's questions.

[The prepared statement of Mr. Escalanti follows:]

PREPARED STATEMENT OF HON. KEENY ESCALANTI, PRESIDENT, FORT YUMA QUECHAN INDIAN TRIBE

Introduction

My name is Keeny Escalanti, Sr., and I serve as the President of the Quechan Tribe of the Fort Yuma Indian Reservation ("Tribe"). I would like to thank the Committee for the opportunity to share our perspective on how Indian gaming has furthered the Tribe's right to sovereignty, self-governance and self-determination and at the same time provided an avenue for building stronger partnerships with local governments and members of our local communities.

The Fort Yuma Reservation encompasses approximately 45,000 acres (approximately 68.7 square miles) with a land base that is located in both California and Arizona, and which shares a border with Mexico. Our Tribal enrollment is approximately 3,900 members.

According to our creation story, our people pronounced "KWAT'SAN", have lived in the Southwest's Colorado River Valley since time immemorial. We are well known for our distinct language, the Yuman, which is a native dialect of the HOKAN Language from modern day California and Arizona. Our Tribe's governing body—the Tribal Council—consists of a President, Vice-President, and five Council Members at large. The President and Vice-President serve four-year terms and the Council Members serve two-year terms.

Our Tribe is largely an agricultural community, driving economic development, in part, through the lease of thousands of acres of Tribal land for agricultural purposes. In addition to agriculture, our Tribe relies on tourism and, of course, gaming to augment our economy.

Our rural location presents unique issues that historically we have struggled to address. We have limited economic opportunities as well as limited access to social services programs that are readily available and accessible to tribes in metropolitan areas. However, with gaming, we have witnessed an increase in the opportunities that we can offer not only to our Tribal members, but also to the non-native residents of our local communities. We have witnessed how the revenue generated from our gaming operations has allowed our Tribe to invest in our local community, thereby fortifying the partnerships the Tribe maintains with our local governments and improving the livelihood of non-member residents. We are not alone, as states are also beginning to recognize how tribes are becoming the strongest allies and benefactors to both local governments and local residents. The Tribe's new Compact with the State of California exemplifies this shift in thought.

Tribal-State Compacts: Recognizing the Importance of Reinvesting in Local Communities

In an effort to strengthen the Tribe's social and economic conditions on our reservation, the Tribe entered into gaming compacts with both California and Arizona pursuant to the Indian Gaming Regulatory Act (IGRA). Today, the Tribe operates one casino in each of these states.

In California, the Tribe controls and operates the Q Casino Resort located near the township of Winterhaven in Imperial County, California. The Q is a state-of-the-art casino resort featuring 1,000 slot machines, 15 table games, live poker, a high limits room, and 166 resort guest rooms.

The Tribe entered into its first compact with California in 1999, authorizing the operation of our first California casino. This compact authorized a relatively modest gaming operation consisting of up to 350 gaming devices. Due to the success in this endeavor, the Tribe moved forward with a resort expansion plan, relocating from the original building to a new facility constructed along Interstate 8 (I–8) highway approximately 1 mile from the Andrade Port of Entry, also located on the reservation.

To that end, in 2006, the Tribe negotiated an amendment to the existing 1999 compact which was signed by then California Governor Gray Davis (the "2006 Amendment"). The 2006 Amendment was signed by Governor Arnold Schwarzenegger. This Amendment authorized the expansion of our California casino, permitting up to 1,100 devices. However, even though the 2006 Amendment authorized the operation of additional devices in our California casino and propelled its relocation, the 2006 Amendment included some unfavorable revenue-sharing provisions which caused the Tribe financial distress. The unfavorable revenue-sharing provisions, coupled with the significant debt we incurred to finance the construction of the new casino facility, deprived our Tribe of the ability to provide essential services to our members and, furthermore, restricted any significant investment in the communities surrounding our reservation.

To alleviate the financial hardship that we experienced under the 2006 Amendment, our Tribe recently negotiated a new Tribal-State Compact with Governor Edmund G. Brown ("2017 Compact"). Governor Brown's administration worked tirelessly to finalize our new compact, allowing the parties to reach an agreement in August 2017, in time for the California Legislature to ratify the compact before the end of this year's legislative session. The Tribe commends and is grateful for the hard work exhibited by Governor Brown and his administration. We are pleased with the terms of our new compact, as it allows for an expansion of gaming devices while offering up more favorable revenue-sharing provisions for the Tribe that will allow it to improve its financial status and augment services that we can provide its membership.

The 2017 Compact is unique in that the State recognizes the benefits of reinvesting gaming revenues in the local community and recognizes the Tribe as a significant contributor to the local economy. For example, under the new provisions, the Tribe is exempt from certain burdensome and counterproductive state based revenue-sharing contributions, allowing the Tribe to reinvest their resources to provide programs to tribal members and local non-native residents, as was expressly recognized during the ratification process the Governor's office as well as members of the California State Legislature.

In addition to removal of certain revenue sharing requirements, the 2017 Compact provides credits counted against required payments to the State if the Tribe invests in certain local programs. For example, the Tribe received credits for non-gaming related capital investments and economic development on or off tribal trust lands, including lands which border the State and also for payments to support operating expenses and capital improvements for non-tribal governmental agencies or facilities operating within Imperial County. Thus, rather than having gaming revenue go to the State, the Tribe, which is in a much better position to understand the unique needs of Imperial County and the surrounding areas, can make a determination as to how to invest gaming revenue into specific County programs and economic development projects around its reservation.

What is particularly striking about the 2017 Compact is that the State seems to recognize, particularly with rural tribes, that boundaries separating local, state and tribal jurisdictions become less relevant as residents travel long distances, often traversing state boundaries, in search of economic and social opportunities—those being scarcer in agricultural communities. The new compact recognizes that the Tribe's economic investments in say, Yuma, Arizona, could have a beneficial impact on those residents of Imperial County. For example, the City of Yuma offers, among other activities, the Yuma Art Center and Historic Yuma Theater, as well as shops, restaurants, wineries and breweries located in Historic Downtown Yuma; all are potentially investment opportunities that the Tribe wishes to pursue, and is now incentivized to pursue, under the more favorable provisions of the 2017 Compact. The Tribe's economic investments in Yuma will benefit the residents of Imperial County because they, having limited options, regularly avail themselves of the opportunities and benefits Yuma has to offer.

In Arizona, the Tribe owns and operates the Paradise Casino, located in Yuma County, Arizona. The Tribe negotiated its Tribal-State Compact with Arizona in 2002 ("2002 Compact"). The 2002 Compact authorized the operation of 566 gaming devices. Paradise Casino currently offers Class III gaming with 480 slot machines, restaurant, bars and an event center which is also used as an emergency shelter in those instances.

The Tribe is currently in the process of negotiating a new compact with State of Arizona, and is hopeful that Arizona will also continue to recognize and appreciate the beneficial impact gaming revenues have on local rural communities.

Strengthening Bonds: Building Stronger Partnerships With Local Governments and Improving Our Local Communities

Gaming is a critically important component of the Tribe's economy. Indeed, gaming has directly or indirectly improved the Tribe's well-being by nearly every measurable standard, thereby furthering the longstanding federal interest in promoting tribal self-determination and economic self-sufficiency. More broadly, gaming has also improved the well-being of the surrounding area—on- and off-reservation—through job creation and local investment, as well as through providing the Tribe with resources to collaborate with local, state and federal agencies to improve the safety and security of the entire community.

Our gaming enterprises have provided significant employment opportunities for both Tribal members and local community members, making our Tribe a significant contributor to the local economy. The Quechan Casino employs over 500 individuals from Imperial County, California, which has a relatively high 24 percent unemployment rate. It attracts employees from as far as Las Vegas, Nevada and San Diego, California. Meanwhile, the Paradise Casino in Yuma, Arizona employs over 150 people from Yuma County, which has an unemployment rate of 16 percent. As the Senator sponsoring the Tribe's California Compact stated, "any job is gold," and the Quechan Tribe is creating work where there was none before.

Gaming has been instrumental in allowing the Tribe to implement community and social services programs for Tribal and community members. Educational programs, for instance, have benefited significantly from gaming revenues, as the Tribe is able to use those revenues to fund scholarships and grants for post-secondary education and vocational programs. The Tribe has also supplemented tribal funding to a program called the Alcohol Drug Abuse Prevention Program (ADAPP), which provides services such as individual treatment plans, clinical assessments, individual sessions, youth group outreach, assistance with special court appearances and transportation.

The Tribe has also implemented programs designed to assist with elder care. The Tribe operates a Senior Center that offers meals and recreational activities to elderly members of the Tribe, other Native Americans in the community, and non-tribal members. The recreational activities that are offered include: Quechan language lessons, sewing, food demonstrations, movies, dancing, exercise classes, local field trips and monthly birthday celebrations. The Tribe also has an Elder Family Services Program, which offers a network of resources for frail elderly and handicapped clients. The program provides support services for the elderly and their families through resource referrals, advocacy, client transportation, case management and family counseling. The program works collaboratively with federal, state, county and city offices and includes a network of the following: Senior Nutrition; Social Services; Indian Health Services; One Stop for Imperial County; Cash Aid Assistance & Food Stamp Program; Social Security; Arizona Native Health Program; and Imperial County Social Services.

Our Tribe is especially proud that we have taken initiative to build the Fort Yuma Health Care Center—which will be operated jointly with the Cocopah Indian Tribe and is scheduled to open in March 2017. The facility will be approximately 76,000 square feet with 22 primary care exam rooms. It will offer clinical, dental and optical health services to both tribal and non-tribal members. It also has the capacity to employ over 176 individuals, although increased federal funding will be necessary to fully staff the facility.

Aside from these economic benefits, the Tribe has also been able to utilize gaming as a springboard to establish strong intergovernmental relationships to ensure the safety and well-being of the broader community. At the local level, in California, the Tribe has a strong relationship with Imperial County's law enforcement and fire prevention agencies, and the strength of that relationship is attributable to the parties' commitment to improving the safety and protection of the local community through frequent communication and financial assistance provided by the Tribe. Pursuant to certain Memoranda of Understanding ("MOUs"), the Tribe pays approximately $400,000 annually to the Imperial County Fire Department and

$214,100 annually to the Imperial County Sheriff Department. Gaming is a critically important contributing factor to the success of this intergovernmental relationship, as the Tribe's ability to meet its financial obligations under these MOUs is dependent upon the success of its gaming enterprises. Again, the California Compact recognizes this symbiotic relationship by allowing the Tribe to credit its financial assistance against monies otherwise due to the State.

At the federal level, the Tribe uses its unique location as an opportunity to strengthen relations and opportunities with federal government agencies. Our Tribe is one of only two tribes that has a port of entry—the Andrade Port of Entry—on our reservation. Our Tribal Fish and Game and Tribal Police Department works collaboratively with the United States Border Patrol on issues of border protection and homeland security. Public safety is the Tribe's highest priority whereas our Tribal Federal Officers work closely with Border Patrol and the revenue derived from our casinos may allow us to do more to further this compelling security interest in the future.

Conclusion

In sum, tribal gaming revenue, when left in the tribal and surrounding communities, creates far more opportunities to those communities than it would through State-managed revenue programs. Rural tribes are uniquely poised to understand the needs of their communities and are thus in the best position to determine how to appropriately invest gaming revenues to address those specific needs. In looking ahead over the next 30 years, our Tribe is hopeful that more States recognize the advantages from, and opportunities created through, the use of gaming revenue by rural tribes—not only for tribal members, but also for those local rural communities.

We thank the Committee for its consideration of these issues important to the Quechan Tribe and to all of Indian Country. I would be happy to answer any of the Committee's questions.

Senator UDALL. [Presiding.] Thank you very much, President Escalanti.

I see we have been joined in the audience by President Begay. He represents the Navajo Nation, the biggest Indian tribe area wise in the Country in three States, but we claim him in New Mexico.

Chairman Frank, please proceed.

STATEMENT OF HON. HAROLD "GUS" FRANK, CHAIRMAN, FOREST COUNTY POTAWATOMI COMMUNITY

Mr. FRANK. Thank you. Good afternoon, Chairman Hoeven, Vice Chairman Udall and other distinguished members of the Committee.

Thank you for inviting me to speak today on behalf the Forest County Potawatomi Community. I am Harold "Gus" Frank, Chairman of the tribe.

We have a diverse set of businesses that allow us to create opportunities for our people and local communities, including two casinos. The Potawatomi Business Development Corporation, our economic development and investment company.

We closely follow new trends and potential threats in the business world. One of the greatest risks facing businesses, including tribal gaming, is the growth of cyber crime. All organizations and companies are at constant risk of cyber theft. Tribal operations are no different.

Improving cyber security controls is crucial to the continued success of Indian gaming. The integrity and future of the gaming industry depends on protecting our systems. We need to be proactive, not reactive, when it comes to defending against cyber crime.

One of our tribe's most important investments over the last several years has been the improvement of cyber security protection at our tribal casinos. Although our casinos have been compliant with applicable State and Federal regulations, we feel the need to go beyond what is required by the minimum standards to protect ourselves from cyber threats.

Therefore, we hired a third party security company to audit our cyber security protection. Following the audit, we invested millions of dollars to upgrade our systems. Some of the things we did include: hiring a security consultant to help us improve our systems and processes; upgrading all credit card machines, ATMs and software to the latest pay card industry standards; purchasing security software that constantly looks for and addresses attacks; creating a new security director position to monitor and safeguard our data; improving employee knowledge of the risk of cyber attacks and teaching them how to spot and respond to attacks; and planning regular security audits to make sure our defenses are working while finding new ways to improve.

We also have gained experience with the Potawatomi Business Development Corporation. One of the company's we own through the Development Corporation is Data Holdings, a leading data center located in Milwaukee.

We store data for a wide range of companies which requires the businesses to be compliant with various internal control standards such as HIPPA and PCI standards.

In addition to the data center, PBDC also owns Redhawk Network Security, a cyber security firm that monitors crime networks and provides security support. Running the data center and Redhawk has given us a valuable perspective on the level of protection required to protect the tribe's businesses from cyber threats.

At the end of the day, in order to preserve the integrity of tribal gaming, our guest and our employee information must be protected from cyber attack. Therefore, proactive measures need to be taken by all tribal casinos. To assist tribes, the National Indian Gaming Commission should provide guidance on internal control standards for Class III gaming that reflects the threats of today. NIGC has been working on this issue and has asked tribes for input on the matter.

Our gaming commission has responded by providing specific recommendations for NIGC to consider. With the growth of cyber crime, we respectfully request that NIGC take special care to examine controls over cyber security.

Concerning our expertise in managing the protection of data for ourselves and others, we would like to offer any assistance we can as the NIGC updates their guidelines. Indian Country and regulators need to be proactive to protect against cyber crime. Doing so will help tribal governments ensure their long term success. Information security is crucial to the future of tribal gaming. The time to act is now.

Thank you, Mr. Chairman and Mr. Vice Chairman, on behalf of the Forest County Potawatomi.

[The prepared statement of Mr. Frank follows:]

PREPARED STATEMENT OF HON. HAROLD "GUS" FRANK, CHAIRMAN, FOREST COUNTY POTAWATOMI COMMUNITY

Good afternoon Chairman Hoeven, Vice Chairman Udall, and other distinguished Members of the Committee. I am Harold Frank, Chairman of the Forest County Potawatomi Community (FCPC). Thank you for the invitation to appear before you on behalf of our Tribe. We appreciate the Committee's initiative in examining and preparing for the future of Indian Gaming.

The FCPC are one of eight Potawatomi bands in the United States. Our ancestral and treaty territory homelands extend from about what is now northern Indiana to the northern shores of Lake Michigan, through present day Chicago and Milwaukee.

Through revenues from a wide array of business interests, we have been fortunate enough to invest in the health, wellness, education, environment and future of our people. Among the diverse set of businesses we own are two casinos in Wisconsin and Potawatomi Business Development Corporation (PBDC).

One of the FCPC's most significant and important investments in recent years has been the modernization and enhancement of internal controls regarding cybersecurity at our casinos. It seems that every week we hear increasingly disturbing news of cyberattacks and data breaches across all industries. All organizations are vulnerable to the theft of confidential data, including casinos.

Improving controls related to cybersecurity is crucial to the future success of Indian gaming. The cost of addressing a single data breach has grown to around $4 million per incident.[1] In addition to the financial cost of being hacked, an immeasurable impact lies in the shaking of consumer confidence. The integrity and future of the gaming industry depends on mitigating the risks posed by cyber threats.

Cybersecurity Investments

Our casinos have always been compliant with the National Indian Gaming Commission's (NIGC) regulations governing internal controls, which include minimum standards for the security of sensitive data.[2] In fact, our tribal-state compact with Wisconsin requires that our minimum internal control standards (MICS) are at least as stringent as the Commission's regulations.

However, we recognize the wisdom of going beyond what is required by law in order to protect ourselves and our patrons from cyber theft. In these efforts, the FCPC took a large, proactive step to improve the level of cybersecurity protection at our casino enterprises by hiring a vendor to conduct a 3rd party security assessment to identify vulnerabilities and consult on any potential risks. Following that audit, our tribe invested millions of dollars to develop and implement sophisticated protections against cybercriminals. The overall takeaway was to move the network and infrastructure into high security zones through modernization. We added layers of security protection to address various threats and vulnerabilities. Some specific actions taken as a result of the assessment include:

- *Hiring a 3rd party security consultant, to assist in addressing areas of opportunity highlighted by the audit.* The FCPC hired a 3rd party security consultant to ensure that audit takeaways were thoroughly evaluated and sufficient action taken to protect from cyberattacks. The consultant has been closely involved with developing standards for IT security personnel, testing the efficacy of implemented controls and ensuring that adequate measures are taken to protect against a breach. The assistance of a 3rd party consultant has been crucial to ensuring strong controls are implemented and updated.

- *Upgrading credit card machines, ATMs and associated software to adhere to and comply with Payment Card Industry (PCI) standards.* When considering industry frameworks governing the protection of sensitive data, we found that the greatest level of protection can be achieved by adhering to PCI standards. As a result, we've invested in hardware that is compliant with PCI standards and offers the highest level of protection to our patrons. All credit card machines now have chip readers with encryption, per PCI requirements, whether they are customer facing or used by employees.

- *Purchasing and implementing security monitoring software to identify, isolate and address any attempts to compromise company systems.* Constant surveillance of company systems is crucial to recognizing and foiling an attack. There are numerous software-as-a-service vendors who offer products to assist in this

---

[1] (June 15, 2016). IBM & Ponemon Institute Study: Data Breach Costs Rising, Now $4 million per Incident. *Press Release, IBM Security.* Retrieved from *http://www.prnewswire.com/news-releases/ibm—ponemon-institute-study-data-breach-costs-rising-now-4-million-per-incident-300284792.html*

[2] 25 C.F.R. Part 543. The Commission updated these regulations in 2012 and 2013.

effort. Through these products, real-time information is provided on attempts to breach company systems, allowing security personnel to take immediate action. We ensure that any vendor with which we partner is compliant with PCI standards.

- *Creating a new Security Director position, dedicated to safeguarding information technology and sensitive data.* The Security Director is a position dedicated to maintaining data security and will play an important role in developing the orientation curriculum and administering training to new and current employees. The Director will also regularly perform penetration testing, hold multiple security certifications and monitor sensitive company data.

- *Improving new hire and current employee knowledge of the risks of cyberattacks and strategies to defend against them.* As mentioned previously, the Security Director will play a large role in improving the security IQ of new and current employees. The majority of cyberattacks come through social engineering, as criminals seek to identify and manipulate key people into performing compromising actions or divulging confidential information. Ensuring that employees are aware of the strategies cybercriminals may use is an essential part of our information security plan.

- *Planning follow-up IT security audits with a 3rd party to ensure effectiveness of newly implemented security protocols.* An IT security audit involves analysis of procedure documentation, technical controls, personnel interview, physical security reviews among any other elements that affect the effectiveness of an information security program. Scheduling follow-up audits ensures that recently implemented protocols are working properly and are effective. Cybersecurity is an ongoing concern—there is no point at which an organization is done updating systems, as more sophisticated attacks are constantly being developed and executed.

Experience at Potawatomi Business Development Corporation (PBDC)

In addition to our experience operating our casinos, the Potawatomi Business Development Corporation (PBDC) was established in 2002 as the economic development and income diversification business of the FCPC.

Under the PBDC's umbrella of companies is Data Holdings, a leading data center located in Milwaukee, Wisconsin. FCPC opened the $33 million data center in May of 2013 after recognizing the growing importance and business opportunity of safely and securely storing confidential data. We wanted to be industry leaders in the data protection space, so developed the data center as the first wholesale, Tier III Enhanced facility in Milwaukee. The data center is compliant with Health Insurance Portability and Accountability Act (HIPAA) and Payment Card Industry (PCI) standards, which establish minimum controls for the protection of patient health data and the transmittal of credit card information, respectively. This experience has given us a unique and valuable perspective on the importance of internal control standards and the level of protection we should strive for in our other businesses, including our casinos.

In addition to owning and operating the data center in Milwaukee, the PBDC also runs Redhawk Network Security, a cybersecurity firm providing network monitoring and device support services. Redhawk partners with clients to provide them with full-time security oversight and expertise. As part of these ongoing efforts, Redhawk has been developing a modular portal to perform penetration audits on client systems and auto-generate a vulnerability report to identify and address any IT security shortfalls. Our exposure to the unique demands and ever-changing world of cyber security from a vendor's standpoint has expanded and shaped our perspective of what is required to ensure the protection of confidential information.

Recommendation

Among the greatest risks facing the future of Indian gaming is cybercrime. Proactive measures should be taken by all tribal casinos to safeguard valuable company and customer information. Indian gaming has rapidly evolving digital gaming and business systems. As these systems continue to grow, they are becoming ever more interconnected. In addition, Internet-connected fixtures are becoming more common, creating additional opportunities for hackers to gain access to networks and exploit vulnerabilities.

Class II tribal gaming establishments are subject to updated NIGC regulations. However, providing guidance on recommended minimum internal control standards for class III gaming which reflect the threats of today is an important step the NIGC can take to protect against cybercrime and safeguard the future of Indian gaming.

In recent years the NIGC has consulted with tribes about drafting voluntary guidance establishing minimum internal control standards for class III gaming, which were last updated in 2006.[3] The Forest County Potawatomi Gaming Commission has responded to the NIGC's solicitation of input, encouraging the development of current and up-to-date NIGC recommended MICS.[4] As we stated in our past correspondence, the FCPC Tribal MICS are evaluated in comparison with class III MICS adopted by the NIGC as required by our compact with the state of Wisconsin. Therefore, it is in the FCPC's best interest to have current and up-to-date MICS. We continue to support the revision and updating of class III minimum internal control standards, though we recognize that the standards will be considered recommended guidelines rather than required MICS.

However, in the preparation of these guidelines, we respectfully request that a particular focus is given to properly updating the NIGC's recommended MICS regarding cybersecurity protections. Encouraging tribes to be proactive rather than reactive with cybersecurity will help protect the industry from the growing threat of cybercrime. Developing and encouraging a strong security infrastructure will help tribal organizations maintain independency and ensure long-term success.

Information security is an important safeguard that will protect tribal gaming from expanding threats in cybersecurity. Considering our status as the operator of major class III gaming facilities and our expertise in protecting and managing sensitive data for others, the Forest County Potawatomi Community would like to offer any assistance we can provide in the development of NIGC guidance regarding minimum internal control standards on cybersecurity for class III gaming.

Thank you again for the opportunity to testify before the Committee today.

Senator UDALL. Thank you very much, Chairman Frank.

Next, we will go to Chairman Forsman. Senator Cantwell speaks very highly of you. Please proceed.

STATEMENT OF HON. LEONARD FORSMAN, CHAIRMAN, SUQUAMISH TRIBE

Mr. FORSMAN. Thank you.

Good afternoon, Chairman Hoeven, Vice Chairman Udall and honorable members of the Committee.

My name is Leonard Forsman and I have the honor of serving as the chairman of the Suquamish Tribe. I appreciate this opportunity to share Suquamish's story and perspective on Indian gaming.

The Suquamish Tribe resides on the 7,000 acre Port Madison Indian Reservation located on the shores of Puget Sound directly across from Seattle, Washington. We have 1,200 tribal citizens, about half of whom reside on the reservation.

The Tribe is the successor of the Suquamish and the Duwamish people that signed the Treaty of Point Elliot in 1855, which created our reservation. That treaty was signed by Chief Seattle who is buried at the Suquamish.

Prior to gaming, unemployment on the reservation was high, graduation rates were low and there were few economic opportunities for the tribe. We had no tax base to fund government programs and constantly had to find ways to make ends meet because of the Federal Government's chronic under funding of Indian programs.

I was on the tribal council when the tribe made the decision to engage in gaming pursuant to IGRA. We identified a parcel of land

---

[3] *NIGC Consultation Topics,* Draft Guidance on the Class III Minimum Internal Control Standards, National Indian Gaming Commission, Updated December 12, 2016. Retrieved from *https://www.nigc.gov/images/uploads/2016-0912-12%20Consultation%20Briefing%20clean.pdf*

[4] George, K. (Chairperson, Forest County Potawatomi Gaming Commission). Letter to: Stevens, T. (Chairwoman, National Indian Gaming Commission). February 7, 2011. Retrieved from *https://www.nigc.gov/images/uploads/Tribal%20Consultation/Regulatory%20Review%202010-2011/ForestCountyPotawatominoicomments.pdf*

that would become the future home of the Clearwater Casino Resort. The cost of that land was $74,000. Fortunately for us, we had $76,000 in our bank account. This decision was a bet the farm moment that has literally changed my peoples' future.

The Clearwater Casino Resort and the revenue it produces for the tribe has allowed us to reinvest in our people and land. Before gaming, the tribe had very few citizens who held higher degrees but today, I am proud to say that we currently have 50 students in our higher education program.

The tribe has been able to create robust programming for our elders, including housing, meals and health care. We provide health insurance for all of our tribal citizens and offer mental health and substance abuse programs.

We operate the Chief Kitsap Academy, a culturally-centered middle and high school on the reservation. Gaming revenues have allowed us to tackle the challenges that face our people, including a new pilot program that is building tiny houses to fight homelessness.

The tribe has been able to use our gaming revenues to reacquire homelands and restore critical habitat. Like many reservations, our reservation was allotted. In 1904, the tribe held just 36 acres but with our gaming revenues, we have been able to reacquire and place almost 1,300 acres back into trust. Overall, 50 percent of the reservation is now held in trust either by the tribe or tribal citizens.

The tribe also operates a salmon hatchery and invests in rehabilitation of critical habitat which benefits the entire Puget Sound ecosystem.

The Suquamish Tribe has invested our gaming revenues to diversify our economy. Today, we operate a seafood company, an 8(a) construction firm, a golf course and several retail stores. The tribe is now the second largest private employer in Kitsap County. We employ 1,400 people between our government and government-owned enterprises. Over 70 percent of these employees are non-tribal and live off the reservation. All of these employees are paid generous wages and benefits.

This story is similar for tribes across the State of Washington where combined we contribute $3.5 billion to the State's gross product and employ more than 27,000 Washingtonians. Indian gaming has also allowed the Suquamish Tribe to take our place in the family of governments. The revenues we created through gaming, the jobs we produce in the community and the investments we have made in our neighbors have helped to usher in a new era in intergovernmental cooperation. We are at the table when important regional decisions are being made and our neighbors welcome our partnership.

Suquamish gaming, like all Indian gaming, is inherently local. We will not pick up and relocate our businesses. We will not abandon our region. We will always be here working to make the regional economy better for our people and our neighbors.

IGRA imposed a structure on Indian gaming and tribes that works. Indian gaming is the most heavily regulated gaming in the United States with three different governments overseeing it. The

Suquamish Gaming Commission is the frontline regulator followed by the NIGC and Washington State Gambling Commission.

In our experience, the three regulators have developed a robust expertise to work together and ensure the integrity of the Indian gaming industry. Any assertion that Indian gaming is lawless or lacks regulation is inaccurate, dangerous and undermines what tribes like mine have worked so hard to build.

While the Indian Gaming Regulatory Act is not perfect, it is working for Indian Country. Gaming remains the cornerstone of Suquamish's economic revival. We are building a sustainable and diversified economy where our people, and the surrounding community have the opportunity to thrive.

Thank you.

[The prepared statement of Mr. Forsman follows:]

PREPARED STATEMENT OF HON. LEONARD FORSMAN, CHAIRMAN, SUQUAMISH TRIBE

Good afternoon Chairman Hoeven, Vice Chairman Udall, and Members of the Committee. Thank you for the opportunity to testify at this important hearing.

My name is Leonard Forsman and I serve as the chairman of the Suquamish Tribe located in Washington state. The Suquamish Tribe is a signatory to the Treaty of Point Elliot of 1855 and a federally recognized Indian tribe. The Tribe has roughly 950 enrolled citizens, half of whom reside on the Tribe's present day homeland on the Point Madison Indian Reservation, which is located just west of Seattle, WA, across Puget Sound.

I am here today to testify about how tribal governmental gaming is working. For the Suquamish Tribe, gaming has helped to revitalize our government, and enable us to invest in the Suquamish people and our future.

Our tribe still faces many challenges, but governmental gaming has brought greater tribal employment, education, economic development, and reacquisition of our reservation lands. As one of the largest employers in our region, government gaming has also given the Suquamish Tribe a seat at the table with our neighboring jurisdictions and governments to discuss shared interests and issues impacting our communities.

Tribal Background

The name Suquamish means "people of the clear saltwater." We are the successor to the Suquamish and Duwamish people.

Chief Seattle signed the Treaty of Point Elliot in 1855, on behalf of the Suquamish and Duwamish—34 years before Washington became the 42nd state. Our people have engaged in commerce on the shores of the Puget Sound since time immemorial.

As is true with many tribes, before we opened our gaming operations, the Suquamish Tribe and our people had few resources and depended almost entirely on the United States to fund our governmental operations and the services we provided to our tribal citizens.

Despite our treaty, federal policies led to the early diminishment of Suquamish landholdings. Beginning in 1886, nearly three-quarters of the reservation was allotted to individual Indians—by 1904, only 36 acres remained in Suquamish tribal ownership, and by 1973, only 37 percent percent of the reservation remained in trust status.

Suquamish Gaming: Robustly Regulated, Government Gaming

Suquamish governmental gaming is subject to a complex regulatory scheme. Unlike statesanctioned gaming, which is subject to regulation by one government, under the Indian Gaming Regulatory Act (IGRA), Indian gaming is regulated by at least two governments, often three. This is substantially more regulation than any other gaming industry. Suquamish governmental gaming is regulated by: (1) the Suquamish Gaming Commission; (2) the National Indian Gaming Commission; and pursuant to a Class III gaming compact with the state, (3) the Washington State Gambling Commission.

In addition, other regulatory bodies regularly engage with Suquamish gaming (FinCEN, IRS, etc.). Consistent with the policy goals of IGRA, this robust regulatory regime ensures that Suquamish gaming is shielded from organized crime and other corrupting influences, that the Suquamish Tribe is the primary beneficiary of

Suquamish governmental gaming, and assures that Suquamish governmental gaming is conducted fairly and honestly for both the Suquamish Tribe and consumers. Each of the three regulating governments now have decades of experience regulating Indian gaming and have largely worked harmoniously to ensure that Suquamish governmental gaming is adequately protected, fair, and honest.

Suquamish Government Gaming: Investment in the Future

The Suquamish Tribe has implemented a three-prong strategy for utilizing our government gaming revenues: (1) economic security for the Suquamish Tribe and our tribal citizens through diversification, investments, and employment opportunities; (2) maintaining a strong tribal government through the provision of programs and services to tribal citizens, cultural enhancement, environmental restoration, and reservation infrastructure; and (3) investment in the reacquisition and restoration of tribal homelands.

Investments in Suquamish Economic Security

Suquamish government gaming is an investment in the Suquamish Tribe, our citizens, and the surrounding community. We have invested millions of gaming revenues into the diversification of Suquamish economic endeavors. Through the Tribe's business arm, Port Madison Enterprises, our economy has expanded beyond the hospitality industry to include: owning and operating a golf course, a spa, and a stand-alone historic banquet facility. This diversification also includes several retail outlets on the reservation, an 8(a) construction company, and a seafood company that is exporting our prized tribal geoduck to markets around the world.

Economic and employment opportunities on the reservation were almost non-existent before Suquamish government gaming but now the opportunity to earn a livable wage is available to our tribal citizens as well as our neighbors. In addition, these investments also provide a pathway for career advancement, which has a cascading effect throughout the broader community.

Investment in Strong Government

As this Committee is well aware, the Federal Government chronically underfunds programs that many tribal nations rely on to provide basic services to their citizens. The Suquamish Tribe uses our government gaming revenues to supplement insufficient federal funds to ensure that Suquamish tribal citizens have access to basic services. This includes funding community health representatives, mental health and wellness services, and drug and alcohol abuse services. We also invest in our elders by providing housing, meals, and health services. And last month, we launched a trial project to provide temporary "tiny homes" for tribal members who otherwise would not have it and connecting them with services provided by the Tribe. This is a more holistic approach that fits with our cultural values and provides flexibility in responding to emergency situations.

Suquamish government gaming revenue has contributed to our longstanding commitment to protecting our treaty resources. This includes operation of our hatcheries, habitat restoration and protection, fin and shellfish monitoring, and other environmental stewardship activities. These investments benefit the Suquamish Tribe and the entire Puget Sound ecosystem.

Suquamish government gaming dollars also helps the Tribe meet our commitment to Suquamish youth. In 2006 the Tribe used our gaming revenues to partially fund the Marion Forsman- Bouchie Early Learning center, which provides early childhood education and child care in a culturally responsive environment for Suquamish and non-tribal community children. We also operate Chief Kitsap Academy, a culturally-centered middle and high school on the reservation. And we are proud that this year more than 50 Suquamish students have enrolled in our higher education assistance programs, which provide aid for students seeking university and technical college degrees and certifications.

Suquamish government gaming revenue helps to continue our connection to Suquamish history, language, and culture. We have been able to fund the construction of a new Suquamish Museum and the House of Awakened Culture, which is a community meeting facility on the shores of Puget Sound. Last year, we opened a community recreation center to foster our community and encourage healthy lifestyles. Suquamish government gaming revenues helped facilitate the return of the Old Man House property to the Tribe (the center of the Suquamish winter village on Agate Pass and Chief Seattle's home that was burned by the United States). In addition, government gaming revenues have helped fund other cultural activities like the annual canoe journey, repatriation of Suquamish remains, and other cultural education and preservation activities

Investment in Suquamish Homeland Restoration

Suquamish government gaming has given the Tribe the opportunity to begin to restore our checkerboarded homelands. Since 1999, the Tribe has worked to consolidate our jurisdiction through acquisition of reservation fee parcels and securing trust status for those parcels (as well as acquiring fractional trust interests from willing sellers). The Tribe now owns undivided interest in 1,331 acres in tribal trust or 17 percent of the reservation. Total trust ownership is 3,893 acres or just over 50 percent of the reservation.

Suquamish Governmental Gaming Has Improved the Surrounding Community

In addition to bolstering the economic outlook for the Suquamish Tribe and our people, Suquamish governmental gaming has proven to be a valuable contributor to the local economy. After Naval Base Kitsap, the Suquamish Tribe is the second largest employer in Kitsap County. The Tribe and our enterprises employ almost 1,400 people. Over 70 percent of those employees are non-tribal and live off the reservation. The Suquamish Tribe provides our employees with generous wages and benefits.

In addition, the Suquamish Tribe and our economic development agency annually give hundreds of thousands of dollars to non-profit organizations in the region. Over time this equates to millions of dollars into local causes and charities.

Fostering Inter-Governmental Relationships

Prior to Suquamish government gaming, we often were ignored or excluded from decisionmaking in the region. I am proud that today we have taken our place at the table among the family of governments. The Suquamish Tribe now regularly engages in regional and state-wide partnerships to improve the lives of people living in our communities.

Tribal-State Relationships have Improved and Strengthened

When Indian gaming began in Washington state, the tribes and the State were just emerging from years of litigation—and sometimes violence—over tribal treaty fishing rights. IGRA prompted the Suquamish Tribe and the State to engage on gaming issues on a government-to-government basis.

In 1989, Washington and the tribes further improved their relationship with the inking of the Centennial Accord. Now codified into Washington law, the Accord sought to improve State- Tribal relationships by providing a framework for government-to-government interaction, including how state agencies, like the Washington State Gambling Commission, engage with the tribes.

The improved relationship is also evident in the evolution of the tribal gaming compacts with the State. Despite the fact that IGRA intended for the tribes to be the "primary regulators" of gaming on their lands, early compacts took a "one size fits all" approach which often led to tension between the tribes and state regulators due to overlapping regulations. By the late 1990s, the State took a new approach to regulation that respected the distinct strengths and goals of each sovereign, and many of the gaming compacts were amended to reflect a changing approach to regulation.

This transition to mutual respect in regulation has laid the foundation for strengthened government-to-government collaboration—in gaming as well as other areas of mutual interest. For example, the gaming compacts have laid the ground work in Washington for other government-to-government agreements on areas where there had been conflict, such as cigarettes, liquor, and fuel.

One thing we can all likely agree on is that Indian government gaming has provided a strong and consistent source of revenue for tribes to fund their governments and immense community needs.

Over time, the State has come to understand that what is good for Indian gaming is good for the State of Washington. According to a 2010 Taylor Policy Group study, Washington Tribes (1) contribute more than $3.5 billion to Washington's gross state product, (2) employ more than 27,000 Washingtonians in tribal casinos and tribal enterprises, including 18,000 non-tribal employees, and (3) generate $255 million in tax revenue for the State and local governments with taxes paid by suppliers and employees.

Indian Government Gaming is an American Success Story

Indian government gaming is working for the Suquamish Tribe and is benefiting our neighbors in Washington state. The Tribe is making significant contributions to Washington's economy and our businesses are eminently local. The Suquamish Tribe will not pick up and leave for other states—we have always been here. There is no immediate need to change IGRA or how it operates. While gaming remains a cornerstone of Suquamish's economic revival, we continue to diversify our economic footprint in the Puget Sound region. The next thirty years are as unpredictable as the last thirty years since IGRA became law. But at Suquamish, we are building a sustainable, successful economy where our people, and the surrounding community have the opportunity to thrive.

Senator UDALL. Thank you very much, Chairman Forsman for that testimony.

Please proceed, Chairman Stevens.

STATEMENT OF ERNEST L. STEVENS, JR., CHAIRMAN, NATIONAL INDIAN GAMING ASSOCIATION

Mr. STEVENS. Thank you, sir.

I wanted to mention my father was the Mike Andrews of what was then the Senate Select Committee on Indian Affairs many years ago and a good friend of your Uncle Mo. I wanted to mention that as we start.

Senator UDALL. Thank you so much.

Mr. STEVENS. Thank you for allowing me to testify here this morning, Vice Chairman Udall and members of the Committee. I understand they have a vote.

Before I start, I want to briefly reflect on the horrific shooting in Las Vegas on Sunday, Mr. Vice Chairman. I was in Vegas with dozens of tribal leaders there to attend the annual Global Gaming Expo when the shooting occurred. Our chief of staff was on the freeway for about two hours when that happened. I only rested when we could account for her being in her hotel room.

Most of Sunday night and Monday morning, we spent texting and calling to check on our colleagues and also assuring our loved ones that we were safe. I was fortunate to have my wife with me, so I was safe. She told me to stay away from the windows.

We know that at least two young ladies from Indian Country were harmed. One young lady from the Lummi Nation and one from the Salt River Tribe in Arizona both remain in serious condition. NCAI President Brian Cladoosby remains by the family's side in Las Vegas and gave a prayer at the opening of the G2E Conference. Our hearts go out to them and their families and all others afflicted.

From Indian Country perspective, we are sadly not strangers to violence. To answer the violence, we are using technology and improving coordination with State and Federal law enforcement, not only on Indian lands, but in nearby communities.

Our Tribal Gaming Protection Network, made up of tribal gaming professionals, has been in place for ten years. The TGPN has and will continue to provide active shooter training, seminars on security and surveillance, human trafficking and other courses on violence prevention. These trainings are taking place this week at G2E as we speak and through our NIGA Seminar Institute.

I have just a brief word on human trafficking, Mr. Vice Chairman. I am a father of three grown daughters and I have eight granddaughters, so I am particularly concerned about the safety of any one of these young ladies in Indian Country.

I assure you our gaming industry does all it can to stamp out this illegal and immoral activity. Indian Country will remain on the frontlines on these issues.

Unlike the criminal justice system in place on Indian lands, the Indian gaming regulatory system is the exact opposite. It empowers tribes to serve as primary regulators and first responders. Because of the multiple surveillance cameras and security personnel in place, our Indian gaming operations are often the safest locations in tribal communities. Again, we can and we must do more to make our operations safe and secure for our citizens and visitors.

With that, I want to thank you for this opportunity. I know we are here today in part to acknowledge the 30th anniversary of the Supreme Court's historic Cabazon and Morongo decision. The Cabazon court affirmed the inherent right of tribes to conduct gaming free of State interference.

A little more than 30 years later, Indian gaming has responsibly grown into a $31 billion industry that is rebuilding our communities, educating a generation of new Native leaders and providing jobs to hundreds of thousands of American families. I cannot say enough about the investments tribes have made in education. Where 30 years ago, we relied on outsiders to serve as doctors, lawyers and other professionals, today we are educating our young leaders and they are returning to serve their communities.

Just the other day, this girl did not look a day over 25 but was actually in her early thirties, was working on my teeth. Believe me they need some work. I looked up and saw how young she was and I asked where she was from. She told me who her grandmother was. It was an Oneida Nation member. She was a very fine dentist working in the Oneida Nation Health Center. I am very proud of that.

Education is one key to making sure that Indian gaming succeeds for the next 30 years. Another key is for Indian Country to continue to do our job to protect our citizens, our customers, our assets and the integrity of our operations.

Last year, tribes invested $450 million on regulation, employing 7,000 regulators, surveillance officers, security personnel and others. In the midst of a revolution that has brought us FaceBook and Google, the tribal regulators are working hard to stay ahead of the technology curve.

Safeguarding our IT infrastructure against cyber threats is a critical part of tribal gaming operations. We are constantly developing IT personnel to meet the challenges of the new digital world.

Probably the most important key to our future success is for this Committee to begin to debate the fix to the tribal-State compacting process that has been broken for more than two decades. We know this is not an easy fix but we call on your leadership to begin a respectful debate to craft an alternative method with which we can secure Indian gaming for the next 30 years.

Finally, Secretary Zinke has repeatedly said tribal sovereignty must mean something. In some cases, sovereignty means keeping the Federal Government out of the way by reducing laws and regulations. This means respecting Indian tribes just as other governments for the purposes of Federal labor laws.

We thank Senator Moran and this Committee for moving the Tribal Labor Sovereignty Act and we look forward to working with you to see it signed into law. Sovereignty also means respecting tribal decision-making for the emerging gaming markets, Internet, fantasy and sports betting.

Tribes should be free to make their own decisions to legalize or prohibit these new markets and that decision cannot be subject to veto by States. Recently, NIGA established the Sports Betting Working Group that is developing a more detailed position. I look forward to working with this Committee and others on policy proposals as that moves forward. We anticipate that group will be working by the end of the year.

In closing, to truly succeed over the next 30 years, we have to work together in an open and honest dialogue. Indian Country, this Committee, Secretary Zinke and the entire Trump Administration must put our minds together to address the challenges of technology, compacting and these emerging markets so that we can build a better future for our children.

That is where I will leave it, Mr. Vice Chairman. I am prepared to answer any questions. Thank you for your time.

[The prepared statement of Mr. Stevens follows:]

PREPARED STATEMENT OF ERNEST L. STEVENS, JR., CHAIRMAN, NATIONAL INDIAN GAMING ASSOCIATION

Introduction

Good afternoon Chairman Hoeven, Vice Chairman Udall, and Members of the Committee. My name is Ernest Stevens, Jr. I am a citizen of the Oneida Nation of Wisconsin and Chairman of the National Indian Gaming Association (NIGA). NIGA is an intertribal association of 184 federally recognized Indian tribes united behind the mission of protecting tribal sovereignty and preserving the ability of tribes to attain economic self-sufficiency through gaming and other endeavors. I appreciate this chance to provide our views about issues and opportunities to ensure the success of Indian gaming over the next 30 years.

February 25, 2017 marked the 30-year anniversary of the U.S. Supreme Court's historic *California v. Cabazon Band of Mission Indians* decision, which held that state governments could not impose their regulatory gaming laws to stop tribal governments from engaging in gaming to provide jobs and economic opportunity for their communities. In the 30 years since *Cabazon*, Indian gaming has proven to be the single most successful economic development tool for tribal governments in more than two centuries.

As this Committee examines issues and opportunities to help Indian gaming succeed over the next 30 years, we urge you to work with other Committees of jurisdiction to closely examine emerging gaming markets such as Internet gaming, daily fantasy sports, and sports betting. These activities pose both potential expansion opportunities and challenges to existing tribal gaming operations and tribal-state compact agreements. Indian Country will continue to work in partnership with federal and state regulators to stay ahead of the technology curve to protect Indian gaming revenues and the integrity of our operations. Finally, to help Indian Country achieve its full economic potential, we call on Congress to extend the respect for tribal sovereignty and the distinct status of Indian tribes in our federalist system to all areas of federal law. This means treatment of Indian tribes for purposes of federal labor laws, respect for tribes in the U.S. Tax Code, and direct federal investments to address the more than $50 billion in unmet need for infrastructure on Indian lands.

Native Nations In the U.S. Federalist System of Government

As noted above, the Supreme Court's 1987 *California v. Cabazon* decision affirmed inherent rights Indian tribes, as distinct governments, to engage in gaming on their lands free from state interference—even those subject to the Termination era Public Law 83–280. The Court acknowledged that Indian gaming was an exercise of tribal government self-determination and noted that gaming provides the sole source of governmental revenue for some tribes and is the major source of employment for many.

The *Cabazon* Court also reasoned that tribal governments' exercise of sovereignty through Indian gaming aligned with the now longstanding federal policy supporting

Indian self-determination and the goal of encouraging economic self-sufficiency.[1] The Court found particularly persuasive statements from President Reagan's Interior Department supporting tribal government gaming. The Court cited the Reagan Interior Department's March 2, 1983 policy directive, which stated that the Administration would "strongly oppose" any proposed legislation that would subject tribes or tribal members to state gambling regulation. "Such a proposal is inconsistent with the President's Indian Policy Statement of January 24, 1983."

President Reagan's 1983 policy statement discussed the historical recognition and treatment of Indian tribes as sovereigns and reaffirmed the then-existing federal policy supporting Indian self-government:

> When European colonial powers began to explore and colonize this land, they entered into treaties with the sovereign Indian nations. Our new nation continued to make treaties and to deal with Indian tribes on a government-to-government basis. Throughout our history, despite periods of conflict and shifting national priorities, the government-to-government relationship between the United States and Indian tribes has endured. The Constitution, treaties, laws and court decisions have consistently recognized a unique political relationship between Indian tribes and the United States, which this administration pledges to uphold.. The administration intends to. . .remove[e] the obstacles to self-government [that] will be charted by the tribes, not the Federal Government. . .Our policy is to reaffirm dealing with Indian tribes on a government-to-government basis and to pursue the policy of self-government for Indian tribes without threatening termination. . ..

President Ronald Reagan, Statement on Indian Policy (Jan. 24, 1983).

President Reagan's policy statement conforms with historical and foundational treatment by the United States of Indian tribes as separate distinct governments in our federalist system. When the United States formed, it acknowledged Indian tribes as sovereign governments, entering into hundreds of treaties with tribes to establish commerce and trade agreements, form alliances, and preserve the peace. In so doing, the U.S. followed the practice of the nations of England, France, and Spain. The U.S. Constitution affirmed these treaties and the sovereign authority of Indian tribes as separate governments. The Constitution's Commerce Clause also expressly provides that "Congress shall have power to. . .regulate commerce with foreign nations, and among the several states, and with the Indian tribes."[2]

Thirty years ago, the *Cabazon* Court also acknowledged the unique position of Indian tribes as separate distinct governments in the U.S. federalist system of government. Indian Country was encouraged to hear the most junior Supreme Court Justice, Neil Gorsuch, give a nod to this legal status during his confirmation hearings earlier this year. Senator Sasse asked then-Judge Gorsuch a broad question about federalism and the idea of separation of powers. Gorsuch replied as follows:

> We divide power in a way that was quite unique. Federalism. You can think of separation of powers as having a horizontal axis and a vertical axis. So that the federal government has certain enumerated powers and authorities, and what the federal government doesn't enjoy the states do, as sovereigns. In this country as well, we have tribes which also bear sovereignty in our part of the world, and bear recognition as such, and I'm glad to have the opportunity to recognize that fact here as a Westerner.

Statement of Neil Gorsuch before the Senate Judiciary Committee (March 22, 2017).

The State of Indian Gaming: 30 Years Post-Cabazon

A handful of tribal governments in the late 1960s and early 1970s, tired of waiting on the United States to fulfill its treaty and trust obligations, took measures to rebuild their communities by opening the first modern Indian gaming operations. These tribal governments used the revenue generated from Indian gaming to fund

---

[1] President Nixon formally ushered in the federal policy supporting Indian self-determination in a Special Message to Congress on July 8, 1970. He stated, "It is long past time that the Indian polices of the Federal government began to recognize and build upon the capacities and insights of the Indian people. . .. The time has come to break decisively with the past and to create the conditions for a new era in which the Indian future is determined by *Indian acts and Indian decisions*." (Emphasis added).

[2] In addition, the U.S. Constitution refers to tribal citizens in the Apportionment Clause, as "Indians not taxed", excluded from enumeration for congressional representation. The 14th Amendment repeats the original reference to "Indians not taxed" and acknowledges that tribal citizens were not subject to the jurisdiction of the United States. The Constitution also acknowledges that treaties are the Supreme law of the land.

essential tribal government programs, cover the federal shortfalls, and to meet the basic needs of their people. From this point forward, Indian tribes began to take their rightful and historical place alongside the federal and state governments, preserving tribal culture and way of life and caring for and protecting tribal government citizens and residents.

Indian gaming operations were spurred by the forward-looking policies of Presidents Nixon and Reagan. As Tribal Governments began to use their gaming revenues to fund essential governmental services and programs and make "Indian decisions" as President Nixon had foreseen, reservation economies and opportunities began to increase. President Reagan's policy statements and support of tribal economic self-sufficiency helped persuade the *Cabazon* Court to uphold the tribal government exercise of Indian gaming free of infringement from the states.

After *Cabazon*, states and commercial gaming interests urged Congress to reverse the decision. Their primary rationale for opposing Indian gaming was the threat of organized crime. However, this Committee found that after approximately fifteen years of gaming activity on Indian reservations there had never been one proven case of organized criminal activity. Senate Report No. 100–446 at 5 (Aug. 3, 1988). This Committee acknowledged that "the interests of the states and of the gaming industry extended far beyond their expressed concern about organized crime. Their true interest was protection of their own games from a new source of economic competition. . .. [T]he State and gaming industry have always come to the table with the position that what is theirs is theirs and what the Tribes have is negotiable." *Id.* at 33 (Additional views of Senator McCain).

Prior to the Cabazon decision, in 1984, the Interior Department's Deputy Assistant Secretary for Indian Affairs testified to this Committee that approximately 80 tribal governments were engaged in gaming with estimated revenues in the tens of millions. At the time, most tribal gaming operations were run out of temporary pop-up buildings or local tribal gyms. Over the past 30 years since the *Cabazon* decision, Indian gaming has responsibly grown to provide a steady source of governmental revenue for Indian tribes nationwide.

In 2016, 244 tribal governments operated 484 gaming facilities in 28 states, helping Indian gaming grow to $31.2 billion in direct revenues (a 4.4 percent increase over 2015) and $4.2 billion in ancillary revenues[3] for a total of $35.4 billion in total revenues. Without question Indian gaming has been and continues to be the most successful tool for economic development for many Indian tribes in over two centuries.

Many tribes have used Indian gaming revenue to put a new face on their communities. Tribal governments have dedicated gaming revenues to improve basic health, education, and public safety services on Indian lands. We have used gaming dollars to improve tribal infrastructure, including the construction of roads, hospitals, schools, police buildings, water projects, communications systems, and so much more.

Indian Gaming and Job Creation

For many tribes, Indian gaming is first and foremost about jobs. While Indian gaming has provided a significant source of revenue for some tribal governments, many tribes engaged in Indian gaming continue to face significant unmet needs in their communities. For these communities, Indian gaming and its related activities have brought the opportunity for employment to Indian lands that have been without such opportunity in recent memory.

Nationwide, Indian gaming is a proven job creator. In 2016, our industry generated more than 310,000 direct jobs. When indirect jobs are included, Indian gaming employs nearly 700,000 Americans. Indian gaming has provided many Native Americans with their first opportunity at work at home on the reservation. Just as importantly, jobs on the reservation generated by Indian gaming are bringing back entire families that had moved away. Because of Indian gaming, reservations are again becoming livable homelands, as promised in hundreds of treaties. These American jobs go to both Indians and non-Indians alike.

Indian Gaming Regulation

Tribal governments realize that none of these benefits would be possible without a strong regulatory system to protect tribal gaming revenues and preserve the integrity of our operations. The regulatory system established under IGRA vests local tribal government regulators with the primary day-to-day responsibility for regulating Indian gaming operations. No one has a greater interest in protecting the in-

---

[3] Ancillary revenues include hotels, food and beverage, entertainment, and other activities related to a tribal government's gaming operation.

tegrity of Indian gaming and our assets than tribal governments. While tribes take on the primary day-to-day role of regulating Indian gaming operations, IGRA requires coordination and cooperation with the federal and state governments to make this comprehensive regulatory system work.

This comprehensive system of regulation is expensive and time consuming, but tribal leaders know that a successful operation relies on strong regulation. In 2016, tribes spent more than $449 million on tribal, state, and federal regulation:

- $336.5 million to fund tribal government gaming regulatory agencies;
- $90.4 million to reimburse states for state regulatory activities negotiated and agreed to pursuant to approved tribal-state class III gaming compacts; and
- $22.2 million to fully fund the operations and activities of the National Indian Gaming Commission.

Tribal, state, and federal regulators work together to maintain the integrity of Indian gaming operations, the security of our patrons and visitors, and Indian gaming revenues. There are approximately 6,000 tribal gaming regulators serving as the primary regulators of Indian gaming.[4] The number of personnel at the state level dedicated to Indian gaming regulation varies from state to state, but it is estimated that 24 states employ nearly 1,000 regulators at the state level.[5]

At the federal level, the NIGC employs approximately 131 regulators and staff in Washington, D.C. and in their various field offices. In addition to the NIGC, tribal governments work with the FBI and U.S. Attorneys offices to investigate and prosecute anyone who would cheat, embezzle, or defraud an Indian gaming facility—this applies to management, employees, and patrons. 18 U.S.C. § 1163. Tribal regulators also work with the Treasury Department's Internal Revenues Service to ensure federal tax compliance and the Financial Crimes Enforcement Network (FinCEN) to prevent money laundering. Finally, tribes work with the Secret Service to prevent counterfeiting.

Today, safeguarding gaming systems and supporting IT infrastructure is a critical part of all tribal gaming operations. Our cybersecurity challenges are essentially no different than other governments and large businesses in that we must defend against a variety of cyber threats on a daily basis-malware, ransomware, external attacks on our networks, and potential malicious insiders. Indian gaming operations employ and develop skilled and qualified IT professionals to manage our IT environments. Many possess the same IT and security certifications such as Network+ and CISSP required by DOD and other Federal Agencies. We acknowledge the need to continually develop IT personnel to meet the future challenges and threats of an increasingly digital world.

Technology also plays a major role in our capability to protect, detect and respond to a variety of cybersecurity events. Like other enterprises, our defenses also include a layered approach to protect networks, servers, and data. Many fundamental controls such as patch management, least privileged access controls, and network segmentation continue to be very effective at protecting systems. However, we also employ other technologies to enhance those protections such as automated vulnerability scanning processes to identify and eliminate security weaknesses. Tribal regulators are also utilizing next generation firewalls and intrusion protection systems to automatically detect and prevent malicious activities on the networks, as well as active malware detection systems and advanced threat defenses to add additional layers of protections to server based systems. Commercial 24x7 security operations centers that continuously analyze logs from firewalls and other critical systems issue alerts whenever anomalous activities are detected. In addition, critical systems are continuously synchronized with redundant systems at hot-site locations to provide high availability and a supplement to traditional backups. Indian Country will continue to invest, adapt, and develop an increasingly stronger and more resilient security posture in response to the current and future cybersecurity threat environment.

NIGA applauds the NIGC and Chairman Chaudhuri for establishing its Division of Technology and for the technical assistance that the Commission provides to all tribal government gaming regulators to identify and eliminate or reduce cybersecurity vulnerabilities. Working together we are staying ahead of the tech-

---

[4] NIGC Budget Justifications and Performance Indication FY18 at NIGC-2; https://www.doi.gov/sites/doi.gov/files/uploads/fy2018_nigc_budget_justification.pdf

[5] At least four of the 28 states that have Indian gaming operations within their borders have refused to negotiate a Class III gaming compact with tribal governments, and thus, do not play a role in regulating Class II gaming.

nology curve to sustain responsible growth and security of tribal gaming operations nationwide.

Finally, in light of the horrific shooting this past Sunday night that involved the Mandalay Bay casino in Las Vegas, it seems appropriate to briefly discuss the work that tribal governments and regulators do to ensure the health and public safety of our patrons and visitors. Of the thousands of personnel dedicated to Indian gaming regulation, many are public safety and security officers. We cannot stop every random senseless act of violence, but we acknowledge that more can and must be done to prevent crime on Indian lands.

Sadly, Indian Country is no stranger to violence. Through more than a dozen oversight hearings that led to the development of the Tribal Law and Order Act of 2010 (TLOA), this Committee highlighted the complex system of justice in place on Indian lands that has led to a crisis of violent crime that has persisted for decades. The Committee report to TLOA "found that the divided system of justice in place on Indian reservations lacks coordination, accountability, and adequate and consistent funding."

Indian Country is doing our part to improve coordination and cooperation with state and federal law enforcement to protect our communities. This coordination includes cross-deputization agreements and special law enforcement commissions that empower officials to investigate and make arrests of suspects regardless of their race or which government's law is implicated.

IGRA vests local tribal government regulators with the primary day-to-day responsibility for regulating Indian gaming operations. This system stands in stark contrast to the failed system that continues to plague criminal jurisdiction in Indian country, where Native communities are often forced to rely on federal officials who are often located hundreds of miles from the Indian lands they are sworn to protect and serve. Despite reforms sought through TLOA, the system of criminal justice in Indian Country is a proven failure. We call on the United States to do more to provide all tribal governments with sorely needed resources to hire tribal justice officials, including police officers, court officials, detention personnel, and mental health counseling to prevent crime on Indian lands—as well as the equipment needed to do their jobs.[6]

This system of comprehensive multi-layered system of regulation is costly has proven itself year after year. The funding, equipment, and personnel dedicated to Indian gaming regulation at the tribal, state, and Federal Government levels far outpace state and commercial gaming regulators. I challenge anyone to compare these numbers and resources to any form of gaming worldwide.

The credit for this system goes to the tribal leaders who make the decisions to fund this system and to the thousands of men and women who have devoted their lives to protecting tribal assets and the integrity of our operations.

Indian Gaming: The Next 30 Years—Issues and Opportunities

Issues and Ongoing Concerns

NIGA is confident that the next thirty years will see Indian gaming maintain steady responsible growth that will further empower tribal communities. Just as much has changed since the Supreme Court's historic *Cabazon* decision in 1987, Indian Country will continue to adapt, anticipate future changes, and make our own positive change to advance tribal sovereignty and tribal government self-sufficiency. One change that NIGA will continue to work for is the longstanding need to restore balance to the IGRA tribal-state compacting process.

Restore Balance to the Tribal—State Compacting Process

As Congress debated IGRA in the mid-1980s, tribal-state relations were combative, with state governments joining forces with commercial gaming interests to limit or put a stop to Indian gaming through legislation and litigation.

Many prominent tribal leaders opposed IGRA because of the class III compacting process, which required tribal governments to engage in negotiations with states in order to conduct Class III gaming. After *Cabazon*, many tribal leaders viewed the compacting process as a limitation on inherent tribal government rights to engage in Indian gaming free of state control affirmed in the Supreme Court's 1987 decision.

In addition, many tribes did not trust that state governments would respect their obligations to negotiate in good faith, or more fundamentally-negotiate. Members of

---

[6] Indian Country fully supports the Department of Justice FY18 Budget, which proposes a 7 percent set aside for Indian tribes from all DOJ Office of Justice Programs accounts and a 5 percent set aside for tribes from the Crime Victims Fund to provide shelters, medical and mental health counseling, and other services to the far too many victims of crime on Indian lands.

this Committee shared tribal leader concerns. This Committee's Report on IGRA sought to alleviate these concerns:

> Under this Act, Indian tribes will be required to give up any legal right they may now have to engage in class III gaming if: (1) they choose to forgo gaming rather than to opt for a compact that may involve State jurisdiction; or (2) they opt for a compact and, for whatever reason, a compact is not successfully negotiated. . ... Thus, given this unequal balance, the issue before the Committee was how to best encourage States to deal fairly with tribes as sovereign governments. The Committee elected, as the least offensive option, to grant tribes the right to sue a State if a compact is not negotiated and chose to apply the good faith standard as the legal barometer for the State's dealing with tribes in class III gaming negotiations. . ..

Senate Report 100–446, at 15 (Aug. 3, 1988).

IGRA envisioned that tribal and state leaders would come together in the best interests of their citizens and their governments to negotiate and reach agreements on class III gaming compacts. In some cases, these compact negotiations were exhaustive, time consuming and costly to both parties. In some case, they have gone smoothly. In those instances, the agreements reached have greatly benefitted the tribal, state, and local governments involved.

In a few unfortunate cases, tribal-state compact negotiations have yet to even take place.

This compromise and the balance that it struck were short-lived. Eight years after enactment, the U.S. Supreme Court destroyed any balance to the IGRA compacting process in its 1996 decision in *Seminole Tribe of Florida v. Florida*. The Court held that Congress did not have the power to waive the states' 11th Amendment sovereign immunity from suit in federal court to enforce IGRA's good faith compact negotiation obligation.

In large part because of the *Seminole* decision, we are concerned that in some situations, the tribal-state compacting process is beginning to deteriorate. Some states are using the imbalance to abuse the compacting process beyond what this Committee intended. Without a method to enforce the state's obligation to negotiate or renegotiate compacts in good faith, many tribal governments are left with the no-win proposition of either not moving forward on a project that could be its only source of non-federal revenue or agree to compact provisions that directly violate IGRA in the form of revenue sharing that amounts to nothing more than direct taxation or concessions that go beyond the regulation, licensing or enforcement of Indian gaming as set forth in IGRA.[7]

As former Assistant Secretary for Indian Affairs, Kevin Washburn, stated, "the Department reviews revenue sharing requirements in gaming compacts *with great scrutiny*." Revenue sharing should only be permitted where a state offers meaningful concessions—such as exclusive rights to offer gaming that provide substantial economic benefits to the tribe.

To prevent any further deterioration of the tribal-state compacting process and to ensure that Indian gaming succeeds over the next 30 years, we urge this Committee to begin the debate to fix this crucial process that has now been broken for more than two decades.

Ongoing Need for a Strong Class II Indian Gaming Industry

In large part because of the Supreme Court's 1996 Seminole Tribe decision, Class II Indian gaming has grown in importance to tribal governments nationwide.

Class II gaming is another aspect of Indian sovereignty that has undergone continuous change and challenges from state governments to the commercial gaming industry. Congress fully intended continuous and positive changes to Class II Indian gaming. IGRA and NIGC regulations define Class II games to include bingo and lotto, and if played in the same location, games similar to bingo—which can be used in connection with electronic, computer, or other technologic aids. Class II games also include nonbanking card games that State law explicitly authorizes, or does not explicitly prohibit, and are played legally anywhere in the state.

This Committee's Report to IGRA clarifies its intent that the definition of class II gaming is not static, and instead must be flexible to enable tribal governments to employ advancements in technology:

---

[7] IGRA did not intend for Indian gaming to help balance state budgets or impose state laws that go beyond the enforcement of gaming-related activities. The Act expressly prohibits states from refusing to enter into a compact "based on the lack of authority to impose a tax, fee, charge or other assessment." *See* 25 U.S.C. 2710(d).

The Committee specifically rejects any inference that tribes should restrict Class II games to existing game sizes, levels of participation, or current technology. The Committee intends that tribes be given the opportunity to take advantage of modern methods of conducting Class II games and the language regarding technology is designed to provide maximum flexibility. In this regard, the Committee recognizes that tribes may wish to join with other tribes to coordinate their class II operations and thereby enhance the potential of increasing revenues. For example, linking participant players at various reservations whether in the same or different States, by means of telephone, cable, television or satellite may be a reasonable approach for tribes to take. Simultaneous games participation between and among reservations can be made practical by use of computers and telecommunications technology as long as the use of such technology does not change the fundamental characteristics of the bingo or lotto games and as long as such games are otherwise operated in accordance with applicable Federal communications law. In other words, such technology would merely broaden the potential participation levels. . ..

Senate Report 100–446, at 9 (Aug. 3, 1988).

From the early 1990s to the mid-2000s, the NIGC and the Justice Department worked against tribal government interests to limit class II Indian gaming in direct conflict with the above-stated congressional intent. The NIGC's own economic impact review found that the Commission's 2007 proposal "would have a significant negative impact on Indian tribes", including decreases in gaming and non-gaming revenue, Indian gaming facility closures, a decrease in jobs, and wide range of broader negative impacts on Native economies.[8]

The NIGC and the Justice Department likewise engaged in a series of federal court cases, seeking to limit the ability of Indian tribes to utilize advanced technology in class II games. Federal courts uniformly rejected these arguments. The Ninth Circuit in *United States v. 103 Electronic Gambling Devices* rejected the Justice Department's antiquated reading of the scope of bingo under IGRA:

The Government's efforts to capture more completely the Platonic 'essence' of traditional bingo are not helpful. Whatever a nostalgic inquiry into the vital characteristics of the game as it was played in our childhoods or hometowns might discover, IGRA's three explicit criteria, we hold, constitute the sole and legal requirements for a game to count as class II bingo. . .. All told. . ..the definition of bingo is broader than the government would have us read it. We decline the invitation to impose restrictions on its meaning besides those Congress explicitly set forth in the statute. Class II bingo under IGRA is not limited to the game we played as children.

U.S. v. 103 Electronic Gambling Devices, 223 F.3d 1091, 1101 (9th Cir. 2000).

The federal courts and public sentiment sufficiently put to rest the NIGC's narrow proposed rule and the Justice Department's dangerous legislative proposal to narrowly interpret class II Indian gaming. The NIGC proposed rules were withdrawn and the DOJ proposal did not gain traction in Congress.

However, as discussed above, the *Seminole* decision destroyed the careful balance that IGRA struck in the class III tribal-state gaming compacting process. This decision has resulted in a number of states that condone and regulate other forms of gaming essentially exercising veto authority over class III Indian gaming. As a result, some tribes rely solely on class II gaming to generate governmental revenue to provide essential services to meet the many needs of their communities.

Indian Country will remain vigilant to ensure that any changes to class II Indian gaming are positive changes consistent with Congress' intent that tribal governments take advantage of the advancing technology to facilitate the play of such games. In recent years, the NIGC and Tribal regulators have worked together to strengthen all regulatory aspects of Indian Gaming. Indian gaming is the most regulated industries in America and we are proud to stand on our record of strong regulation, adaptive technologies, and revolutionary gaming innovations. We look forward to further strengthening class II Indian gaming, changing with advances in technology as this Committee intended over the next thirty years under IGRA.

Emerging Gaming Markets

For nearly two decades, Congress has considered legislation to either expand or prohibit various forms of gaming in the United States. Most of the debate has fo-

---

[8] Meister, "The Potential Economic Impact of the October 2007 Proposed Class II Gaming Regulations" submitted to the NIGC, February 1, 2008. Found at *http://www.nigc.gov/Portals/0/NIGC%20Uploads/lawsregulations/proposedamendments/MeisterReport2FINAL2108.pdf*

cused on Internet gaming. However, in recent years, the discussion has extended to daily fantasy sports wagering and sports betting.

More than 240 tribal governments have made significant investments in their gaming operations based in part federal laws that regulate or prohibit certain forms of gaming. The great majority of these tribal governments have entered into compacts with states that include exclusivity provisions, most often promises on the part of the state to not permit other forms of gambling within the state in return for a portion of the tribal government's Indian gaming revenue.

NIGA, from an organization perspective, does not support or oppose these new markets. However, if Congress does act to establish or prohibit these emerging forms of gaming, we do ask that this Committee work with other committees of jurisdiction over these activities to first consider the impacts on Indian gaming, and work to limit impacts on tribal Indian gaming operations.

While NIGA and our Member Tribes are developing a formal position on sports betting, our existing position on Internet gaming is instructive to all emerging gaming markets under consideration by Congress.

NIGA's Internet gaming principles are directives from our tribal leadership. They are guided by and grounded in NIGA's overall mission to protect tribal sovereignty and to protect rights of all tribes to shape their economic futures. In short, NIGA and our Member Tribes are working to ensure that any federal legislation that authorizes a new form of gambling in the new United States: acknowledge that tribal governments have a right to legalize or prohibit the new activity—not subject tribal eligibility in the new market to a state government's decision to opt-out of the activity; provide all federally recognized Indian tribes with equal access to the new market; acknowledge that tribal government revenues generated from the new market are not subject to taxation, as tribal government revenues are dedicated to the benefit of our communities and thus are 100 percent taxed; and protect existing tribal government rights under tribal-state compacts and IGRA. This basic framework conforms with the U.S. Constitution's recognition of Indian tribes as separate governments as well as the federal policy supporting tribal government self-determination and economic self-sufficiency.

Opportunities: Economic Development Beyond Indian Gaming

All of Indian Country has been and continues to strive for economic self-sufficiency beyond Indian gaming. In my time as Chairman of NIGA, I have worked with our Member Tribes to encourage economic diversification beyond Indian gaming. NIGA is working with our Member Tribes to further encourage tribe-to-tribe giving and lending. Through our American Indian Business Network, we work to highlight Native owned businesses and procurement of Native-produced goods and services. Empowering tribal entrepreneurs and tribal government owned businesses, will help shape our communities and empower the next generation of Native leaders.

While Indian gaming has worked well to empower tribal governments, provide reservation jobs and supplement basic governmental programs and services, far too many tribal communities continue to suffer the devastating impacts of the past failed federal policies. Too many of our people continue to live with disease and poverty. Indian gaming is part of the answer, but we all must do more to reverse these horrific statistics and establish more opportunities for all residents of Indian Country.

Tribal governments need help to fulfill Indian Country's full potential. That potential can only be achieved by reforming and aligning federal laws with the U.S. Constitution's acknowledgment of Indian tribes as separate distinct governments in the United States' federalist system of government. Federal laws and policies should follow a dual purpose of respecting Indian tribes as governments while also working to uphold the federal governments treaty and trust obligations to Indian tribes.[9]

---

[9] Through treaties, tribal governments ceded hundreds of millions of acres of tribal homelands to help build this great Nation. In return, the United States incurred a solemn obligation to provide for the education, health, public safety and general welfare of Indian people. President Nixon embraced these obligations in his Special Address to Congress in 1970 ("The special relationship between Indians and the Federal government is the result of solemn obligations which have been entered into by the United States Government. Down through the years through written treaties and through formal and informal agreements, our government has made specific commitments to the Indian people. For their part, the Indians have often surrendered claims to vast tracts of land and have accepted life on government reservations. In exchange, the government has agreed to provide community services such as health, education and public safety, services which would presumably allow Indian communities to enjoy a standard of living comparable to that of other Americans.").

The Tribal Labor Sovereignty Act

One of the most prominent examples of a federal law's failure to acknowledge Indian tribes as governments is the National Labor Relations Act (NLRA).

In 2004, the National Labor Relations Board (NLRB) reversed decades of its own precedent to apply the NLRA to tribal government enterprises.[10] The NLRB has read the Act's governmental exemption to cover the U.S. federal government, states and political subdivisions (counties, cities, etc.), the District of Columbia, and U.S. territories and possessions—and commercial enterprises owned and operated by these entities.[11] As a result of the NLRB's 2004 decision, Indian tribes are the only form of government in the United States not exempt from the NLRA.

The Board reasoned that "tribal casinos and similar businesses are commercial enterprises in direct competition with similar non-tribal businesses." This is a dangerous misstatement of fact that disrespects tribal sovereignty and ignores the economic realities facing many tribal governments. Tribal Laws require, and Federal Law mandates, that revenues generated from Indian gaming be used entirely for government purposes. Commercial gaming enterprises conversely are for-profit individually owned operations.

With specific regard to Indian gaming, tribal casinos are wholly owned and operated by tribal governments. Tribal governments generally lack an effective tax base—Indian lands are held in trust by the U.S. and cannot be subjected to real estate taxation, high reservation unemployment makes income taxation unworkable, and restrictive Supreme Court rulings have severely limited tribal government sales taxes. For many tribal governments, Indian gaming operations, tribal timber operations, and other tribal government enterprises constitute the sole source of governmental revenue that is used to fund tribal public safety, education, health, housing and other essential services to reservation residents. Ignoring the purpose of tribal government enterprises subjects vital tribal government programs to shutdowns and work stoppages.

Equating Indian gaming to commercial gaming also completely ignores the text and intent of the Indian Gaming Regulatory Act (IGRA). Congress imposed IGRA on Indian gaming operations to establish a system of federal regulation and "to provide a means of promoting tribal economic development, self-sufficiency, and strong tribal governments." IGRA mandates that tribes use revenues generated from Indian gaming for one of five government purposes: to fund tribal government operations, programs, and services; to provide for the general welfare of the community; to promote tribal economic development; to donate to charitable organizations; or to fund local government operations.

NIGA thanks Senator Moran and the co-sponsors of S. 63, the Tribal Labor Sovereignty Act, which would restore acknowledgment of Indian tribes as governments for purposes of the NLRA. We also thank this Committee for advancing the bill in February of this year.

NIGA has made clear from the beginning that this effort to amend the NLRA to restore the longstanding treatment of Indian tribes as other forms of governments is not anti-labor. This effort is purely about respect for tribal sovereignty and the U.S. Constitution's acknowledgement of Indian tribes as separate forms of governments within our federalist system.

Comprehensive Tax Reform

The U.S. Tax Code is also rife with provisions that ignore the federal government's treaty and trust obligation to Indian Country, the federal policy supporting tribal government self-determination and economic self-sufficiency, and the Constitution's recognition of Indian tribes as separate sovereigns—all to the great detriment of Indian Country employment and economic development.

Federal tax policy has a significant and in most cases positive impact on the economies of state and local governments, and U.S. territories. The U.S. Tax Code provides governmental entities with preferred access to capital to finance infrastructure projects, provides tax incentives to individuals and corporations to invest in governmental and economic development projects. Many of these federal tools for

---

[10] See *NLRB Opinion in Fort Apache Timber Co. and Construction* (Oct. 19, 1976)(Holding that a tribal government owned and operated "commercial enterprise" located on Indian lands is not an "employer" for purposes of the NLRA).

[11] The NLRA was enacted in 1935 to address upheavals in private industry. Government employers were expressly exempted from the Act. Although the NLRA did not list all forms of government subject to the exemption, the NLRB has consistently interpreted the government exemption to include the District of Columbia, U.S. territories and possessions, and—until 2004—tribal governments.

governmental economic development are not available to Indian tribes, or require tribes to apply to state governments in order to receive a portion of the benefit.

Rep. Ron Kind (D–WI) and Rep. Lynn Jenkins (R–KS) have sponsored H.R. 3138, the Tribal Tax and Investment Reform Act. The bill acknowledges that Indian tribes face historic disadvantages in accessing the underlying capital to build the necessary infrastructure for job creation, and recognizes that "codifying tax parity with respect to tribal governments is consistent with Federal treaties recognizing the sovereignty of tribal governments."

H.R. 3138 seeks to establish parity for tribal governments with state and local governments for purposes of several provisions in the Tax Code, including: the issuance of tax-exempt bonds for tribal government projects; treatment of tribal government pensions; treatment of tribal government foundations and charities; and acknowledgement of tribal court/tribal government authorized adoptions for purposes of the federal tax credit for the adoption of special needs children; among other items.

The enactment of these provisions will reinforce the governmental status of tribes, facilitate equal access to federal tax and financing tools enjoyed by other governmental entities, and permit tribes to make important investments in their own communities. We understand that a companion bill is under consideration in the Senate and we urge Members of this Committee to support that bill when it is introduced.

I want to highlight two additional glaring examples of the Tax Code's lack of respect for the status of Indian tribes as governments: the federal New Markets Tax Credit and the Low Income Housing Tax Credit. While these federal programs have worked well to incentivize outside investment in state, local, and territorial government housing and economic development projects—they have fallen far short in Indian Country.

For more than thirty years, the Low Income Housing Tax Credit program (LIHTC) has been the most significant producer of affordable housing in the United States. Congress enacted the LIHTC Program in 1986 to provide the private market with greater incentives to invest in affordable rental housing. In 2014, the annual expense credits for the LIHTC program was $6.7 billion, making the program one of the largest corporate tax programs administered by the Federal Government.

All 50 states, the District of Columbia, Puerto Rico, American Samoa, Guam, the Northern Mariana Islands, and the U.S. Virgin Islands receive direct LIHTC allocations, which they competitively issue to developers who construct, rehabilitate, or acquire rental housing for lower-income households. Indian tribal governments are the only sovereign in the United States to not receive a direct LIHTC allocation.

While the Indian Housing Block Grant program and federal housing loan guarantee programs have worked to cut into the housing shortfalls in Indian Country, these programs do not meet the significant housing needs of Indian Country.[12] Providing Indian Country with direct access to LIHTC would significantly improve the ability of Indian tribes to leverage capital from these existing programs and help address the housing shortage on Indian lands.

While individual Native Americans are counted towards a state's population for purposes of the tax credit, the housing projects that stem from the credits have failed in many cases to reach Indian Country. The most common reason that these credits do not reach Indian Country is that state governments do not consider low income housing on Indian lands as an affordable housing priority reflected in the state's qualified allocation plan (QAP), or state QAPs establish criteria and requirements that do not exist in most rural tribal communities—making tribal housing project ineligible to even apply for the credit.

As Congress moves towards comprehensive tax reform this year, we urge this Committee to work with the Senate Finance Committee and others to reform the Tax Code to acknowledge the governmental status of Indian tribes and align it with the federal policy supporting Indian tribal self-government and economic self-sufficiency.

Conclusion

As the *Cabazon* Court acknowledged more than thirty years ago, Indian gaming is Indian self-determination. Less than 18 months later, Congress enacted IGRA in part to foster and strengthen these acts of self-determination. The Act has generally

---

[12] Over 90,000 American Indian families are homeless or under-housed. More than 30 percent of American Indian families live in overcrowded housing—a rate six times the national average. Approximately 40% of Indian Country housing is inadequate according to the federal definition, compared to only 6 percent nationwide. It is estimated that it would take approximately 33,000 housing units on Indian lands to alleviate overcrowding and an additional 35,000 units to replace existing housing in grave condition—at an approximate cost of $33 billion.

delivered on its stated goals of strengthening tribal governments and empowering Indian communities. However, the careful balance struck in IGRA's compacting process is broken and must be addressed to pave a path for the success of Indian gaming's next 30 years.

Indian gaming is one tool that is helping tribal governments overcome decades of injustice. In order to meet the needs of tribal communities, Congress must work to empower tribes with the same tools that other governments are provided under our federalist system, most prominently respect for Indian tribes for purposes of federal labor laws, and tax credits and other incentives to help tribal governments reach their full economic potential.

Chairman Hoeven and Members of the Committee I again thank you for this opportunity, and I am prepared to answer any questions.

Senator UDALL. Thank you, Chairman Stevens, very much. I think it was excellent that you reminded us of *Cabazon* because that is really where we started. That was a historic opinion by the Supreme Court. It affirmed the tribes' right to regulate gaming on tribal lands. The Court recognized that a tribe may engage in gaming if located within a State that permits such gaming for any purpose.

They really recognized the economic part of this and the tribal self sufficiency. In that ruling, which was interesting to me, they preempted the State interest in regulating gaming. That is where we started. Then we went to IGRA and we need to remember that history because that was a very strong opinion by the U.S. Supreme Court.

We heard the National Indian Gaming Commission testify about the balance between States and tribes post-Seminole. Chairman Stevens, in your written testimony you urged this Committee to explore addressing the tribal-State compact negotiation process. What specific recommendations do you have to ensure that tribes and States are on equal footing as intended under IGRA?

Mr. STEVENS. I think we need to rely on our Administration to try to find regulatory solutions for the compacting process. I think it is important, especially with the Pojoaque Pueblo and the Seneca in New York, that we move forward in a good, strong proactive way.

I am glad you mentioned that original court case because we have always worked and moved in good faith. We hope that the States can continue to do that and we can build a stronger relationship because I think we have proven we are safe and secure and do a great job in Indian Country.

Senator UDALL. Thank you so much for that answer.

I do not know if any of the other panelists want to comment on that question? If not, I will move on to my next question.

[No audible response.]

Senator UDALL. Let me move on.

This is for the entire panel. Can you describe how local communities benefit from tribal gaming operations whether through jobs or investment back into the community? Chairman Frank?

Mr. FRANK. Up in northern Wisconsin where our reservation is located, we are the number one employer in the Forest county area. We employ about 600 non-tribal employees out of a county of probably less than 10,000 people combined.

I am proud to say that we are also a major employer in the City of Milwaukee. Of all our employees in the City of Milwaukee, about 80 percent of our employees are minorities. About 65 percent of those minority employees, the other minority group would be single mothers.

How does it benefit the communities? I think it speaks for itself. The packages we have to offer our employees are second to none. Health care is the number one concern. I think we have mightily contributed to the economics of the community.

Senator UDALL. Thank you.

Chairman FORSMAN.

Mr. FORSMAN. I think the biggest investments we have made are not only in jobs and investments in local businesses, but it is also our intergovernmental cooperation. We have strong relationships with the county and the cities and with the State. We are very active in that in a lot of different arenas, habitat protection, water quality but also economic development and trying to manage sprawl and things like that together as we have more and more growth in our area. Those are some.

We also invest a lot in local non-profits in our charitable contributions, as a lot of the tribes do, and are very active in that as well. We are really proud of being able to be one of those emerging and responsible governments looked upon for not only our vision but our values.

Senator UDALL. Thank you.

Mr. Stevens, please.

Mr. STEVENS. Right off the top, 390,000 direct jobs in Indian gaming are a clear reflection, especially in the economy that had its ups and downs over the years. We continue to be not just putting Indians to work but America to work in our industry. If you include the indirect employment, it is well over 700,000 jobs, and safety, education and training and our service agreements that we have developed

My father taught me. I was the stern kid that was talked to about taxation and how I understood sovereignty. My father taught me that service agreements help us all understand one another and help communities work together. It has been 20 years since I listened to my father. The conference that I had to leave with your invitation to come here was my first experience over 20 years ago talking about service agreements and the communities working together.

Again, I have 15 grandchildren. They go to school in a state-of-the-art school classroom and gymnasium. My late grandmother taught there into her nineties. We are doing great things and are a clear reflection of not just Indian Country but the people around us are thriving as well.

Senator UDALL. Thank you very much.

President Escalanti, please.

Mr. ESCALANTI. We too are a tribe that shares all our revenues derived from our casinos. For example, the tribe provides the local fire department with annual payments of $400,000 and the local enforcement agencies with an annual payment of $214,065.

We also provide health insurance for our employees. We are a self insured type of organization that provides these health care benefits to our employees. We are one of the rural tribes that actually provides employment to the surrounding community as far as

Vegas, San Diego, El Centro, Calexico, even across the border, Yuma County, so on and so forth.

Senator UDALL. Thank you very much.

One of the things I think we should not forget, all these good things we have talked about. I am going to ask a bit more about that but we need to remember there is a Federal trust responsibility. There are treaties out there and the Federal Government needs to continue to do the good work there and provide the resources to your tribes and the tribes across the Country to make sure you can continue to improve the quality of life in Indian Country.

I do not think we should ever want to hear the excuse that tribes are doing well with gaming, now we do not need to help them anymore.

We heard today about jobs generated directly from gaming and the billions of dollars of revenue generated but I think we also need to acknowledge that gaming can serve as a catalyst for tribes to diversify their economic portfolios. Tribes are now using the gaming revenue to branch out into other business from cyber security like Forest County Potawatomi to hotels and resorts like Laguna Pueblo in my home State of New Mexico.

This is for the entire panel. Can you discuss how your tribes have used gaming revenues to diversify their business interests?

Mr. FORSMAN. In Suquamish, we have been able to diversify not only in our resort casino, which is becoming a regional destination. We are trying to attract more business from Seattle. We have also invested in purchasing a golf course which was up for tax foreclosure. This was a failing business and we were able to come in, purchase it and restore it to more of a thriving business. There are a lot of residents around there who are very grateful that we acquired it.

We built a brand new clubhouse there and are actually going to host the Senior LPGA tournament there next year. We are pretty excited about that. That should be a great experience for us.

We also have an 8(a) construction firm which does a lot of work for the tribe and also for our local military bases. We have a number of naval bases in our area including Sub Base Bangor and the Puget Sound Naval Shipyard which employs a lot of our people and others in that respect as well.

We have three retail stores on our reservation that sell gasoline, sundries and other products including gasoline and liquor. We have compacts with the State which provides more money for our government activities.

I think the Federal Government's investments in law enforcement, the courts, environmental protection and all those things are vital for us and I believe are some of the best investments and return on the dollar I think the Federal Government gets because the tribes use that money to perform a lot of different services for everyone in our community.

Senator UDALL. Chairman Frank.

Mr. FRANK. How do we use our money to invest and diversify our economy? If you don't mind, I have a little story to tell on this one. Several years ago when we were sitting as the executive council, a guy came in with a proposition to us about a business venture.

I looked around at the executive council and said, how many of us have ever sat and closed a business deal? Not one of us had so we had no expertise on how to do business. We had an attorney general named Jeff Crawford who is a pretty smart fellow.

He said what we need is a business development corporation. That is what got us going on the business development corporation. That corporation is assigned the task that if anything ever happens to gaming, we should be continuing to provide the services a government should provide for its citizens.

We invested in many things. I am glad the chairman mentioned 8(a) because that is one of the things we invested in. We also invested in a bank. There are a number of things we invested in.

All these opportunities we invested in were opportunities which we feel tribal members have an opportunity to work in. With Indian gaming, yes, we have diversified our economy and continue to look for new ventures and new fields to invest our dollars in for our citizens.

The CHAIRMAN. [Presiding.] Mr. Stevens.

Mr. STEVENS. To tag on to Vice Chairman Udall's last question, thank you for your leadership, as he leaves. I just talked about the non-gaming tribes and the non-market tribes. I am glad that we continue to keep them in our hearts and our minds. That is our obligation. For this last question, that is a key component to helping those tribes. Thank you, Mr. Vice Chairman.

I think economic development and individual businesses, tax credits, all these things are key components to helping build a better future for not just gaming but for all of our communities, tribal enterprise or individual tribal businesses.

My daughter and son-in-law are a small business. They work hard at it. It is not easy to do. Where tribes and government can continue to support them, I don't know if it quite lies under the trust responsibility Senator Udall talked a little bit about, but I think it is in our best interest to help create business, not just at the tribal enterprise level, but for our individual tribal members.

We worked with the National Center for American Indian Enterprise Development and the National Congress of American Indians. It is really key. I mentioned we were all in Las Vegas. The G2E is the biggest show in the world. That is where we are exchanging ideas and thoughts and creating business and opportunities for us to move Indian Country forward with and beyond gaming.

You may have read where the Seminoles own the Hard Rock brand and Mohegan is working in South Korea. We really have those kinds of opportunities. If we can partner and help those other tribes build, we can do great things for the next 30 years but we need Congress' support, we need this Administration's support because too many people do not understand Indian tribes as sovereign governments and what we do. The impact we have goes far beyond our reservation boundaries.

We keep helping economically in the United States of America and our benefits go far beyond our reservation boundaries. I wanted to say that regarding that question.

The CHAIRMAN. Certainly.

Chairman Escalanti, can you discuss how the National Indian Gaming Commission has worked to address some of the unique issues in regard to rural gaming, rural tribes?

Mr. ESCALANTI. Chairman Hoeven, it was just brought to my attention yesterday as we were meeting with the congressional leaders that there was a rural committee that actually can assist rural tribes as far as assisting them on their issues and concerns they had.

I really was not aware that the National Indian Gaming had such a rural committee available to assist rural tribes. Therefore, if there are these types of offices, I really do not know where they are located. Most of the time, if we have an issue, our regulatory body or the tribal council goes directly to Indian Gaming headquarters with issues and concerns they have back at home.

The CHAIRMAN. Chairman Frank, in your written testimony you discussed the need for tribes to be proactive in establishing measures to protect and safeguard valuable company and customer information.

It appears it has been several years since your tribe submitted draft cyber security guidance and standards to the NIGC for their comments and feedback. Have you received their comments and feedback on that draft policy that you submitted?

Mr. FRANK. To the best of my knowledge, the answer would be no.

The CHAIRMAN. So you are still looking for some follow-up from the NIGC on your cyber security policy?

Mr. FRANK. Yes.

The CHAIRMAN. Chairman Stevens, how has the continued delay in passing the Tribal Labor Sovereignty Act impacted tribes? As you know, it is legislation we are working on.

Mr. STEVENS. I think it continues to impact us overall in our rights as governments. It is something that is very important to us and helps us to be able to have an even relationship with all other entities.

We are probably the only government that has been subject to this law. I think it kind of sets us back and keeps us kind of treading upward. We continue to advocate that for many years it was always recognized, tribes as governments, in the tribal labor law. It is only recently that we have had to deal with this.

We have been working on it for many years. Everything that we explain to our lawmakers clearly identifies us as governments, governments long before there was even the United States Constitution. It continues to be an uphill struggle. We deal with it proactively and we deal with it in a manner that is non-anti-labor.

I have three uncles, maybe four, I have lost count, but they helped build the Mackinac Bridge, they built the Sears building in Chicago, New York, San Francisco, and Los Angeles. There is a bunch of Native people that built America, so we are not anti-union. We just want to be treated fairly as governments.

The CHAIRMAN. Again, to all of our witnesses, to both the first panel and this second panel, I would like to thank you for being here. We appreciate your written testimony.

Also, we will have the record open for two weeks so that members may submit any written follow up questions for the record.

With that, thanks again not only for you being here but the work you are doing in Indian Country. Thank you so much.

We are adjourned.

[Whereupon, at 4:25 p.m., the Committee was adjourned.]

APPENDIX

Prepared Statement of Hon. W. Ron Allen, Tribal Chairman/CEO, Jamestown S'Klallam Tribe

Chairman Hoeven, Vice-Chairman Udall and distinguished members of the Committee, on behalf of the Jamestown S'Klallam Tribe, I want to thank you for the opportunity to submit this testimony for the record. I am W. Ron Allen and I serve as the Tribal Chairman and CEO of the Jamestown S'Klallam Tribe.

The Jamestown S'Klallam Tribe is located in northwestern Washington State, approximately 70 miles west of Seattle on the Olympic Peninsula. Our Tribal Governmental Campus encompasses an area of 13.5 acres, and the Tribe has an additional 265 acres in trust. We have approximately 600 Tribal citizens.

The name S'Klallam means "strong people" in Coast Salish, and I owe my own existence today to the strength of my ancestors, as well as, the current membership of our Tribe, which embodies strength and resilience. We live on a small amount of land in a rural location, but our strength comes from our ancestral homelands and waters, including the Puget Sound and Strait of Juan de Fuca region. Our Tribe is a signatory to the Point No Point Treaty of 1855 and those lands and waters were included in the negotiations of the Treaty as well as our reserved rights to hunt and fish in our usual and accustomed places. In order to preserve our sovereign rights and remain near our traditional fishing areas, our ancestors purchased these lands in 1874 so that we would not be displaced from our Tribal homelands.

Off-Reservation Fee to Trust Acquisitions and Indian Gaming

The Department of the Interior (the Department) has recently issued an Advanced Notice of Proposed Rulemaking to amend the off-reservation land acquisitions by creating a new two-step process that will require Tribes to address numerous criteria, including gaming considerations that is not currently required. It is a cumbersome and expensive process to place lands into trust so this would be in fact doubling the burden on Tribes in an already burdensome system. In addition, the regulations are overly broad and would allow an opportunity for outside interests to object for any reason at all so the process could be dragged out for many years and cost Tribes an exorbitant amount of money.

The original intent of the Indian Reorganization Act of 1934 (IRA) is to restore Tribal homelands. Between 1887 and 1934, a hundred million acres of Indian land was sold or stolen. The 1934 Act and the intent of the Act should be the primary consideration and criteria that the Department should consider for placing land into trust. The proposed regulations would undermine the intent of the IRA by empowering the State and local governments' interests at the expense of Tribal sovereignty. Tribes can cite numerous instances where local governments have taken active steps to delay and/or halt Tribal land acquisitions and hinder or destroy economic development opportunities.

The Department's proposal improperly inserts gaming considerations into the fee to trust process as prohibited by the Indian Gaming Regulatory Act (IGRA). The Department does not have the necessary land acquisition authority to include this gaming provision in the new regulations. This is already covered by IGRA. It would insert gaming into the 151 regulations and put new hurdles into place for land into trust acquisitions.

Some Tribes, like Jamestown, have small reservations and reservation land or adjacent land acquisitions are not always feasible. Local entities often see our success and try to capitalize on it by increasing the price of their land which essentially locks us out of the market. We have had a lot of success reacquiring our Tribal homelands for a variety of purposes, economic development and job creation, infrastructure development, for cultural purposes and to protect our sacred sites, and to secure our natural resources and Treaty rights. We are excellent stewards of our lands and we don't need other entities telling us what we can and cannot do with our property. We deserve the same respect that is afforded to State and local governments when they make land use decisions for development. The Department should recognize our authority and trust us to carry out our governmental responsibilities.

The Indian Gaming Regulatory Act and Jamestown S'Klallam Gaming

Our treaty is not a granting of rights from the Federal government to the Tribe—it is an expression of sovereignty, a decision to cede certain rights in certain areas in exchange for the reservation of all inherent rights in another area. As a separate sovereign, our Tribe exercises substantial undiminished powers, rights, and responsibilities over its lands and peoples. That includes the right to exercise our self-governing authority to conduct gaming on our land. The Jamestown S'Klallam Tribe is a gaming Tribe.

In 1987 while advocating for the passage of IGRA, Jamestown and seven other Tribes were also working on an initiative to restore relations between Indian nations and the Unites States on a government-to-government basis. Our call for government-to-government relations did not represent any new assertion of Tribal rights. We were merely trying to reclaim the rights reserved by us and guaranteed in treaties with the U.S. government. The Self-Governance Demonstration Project, Title III amendments to P.L. 93–638, the Indian Self-Determination and Education Assistance Act of 1975 (ISDEAA), was that Tribally-driven initiative made possible through Congressional authorization and appropriation support. The amendments were structured to protect the Trust relationship of the United States to Indian people. The goal of the Project was to provide Indian Tribes with the tools and the opportunity to exercise greater control over our affairs and government responsibilities. As one of the original eight Self-Governance Demonstration Tribes in the Department, for the past 30 years Jamestown has administered and managed programs, activities, functions and services more efficiently and effectively than the Bureau of Indian Affairs to better address the local needs of the Tribal citizens, which has also benefitted the surrounding communities. In June 1989, Congress funded the participation of seven more Tribes in the Demonstration Project.

Gaming is not a privilege that has been granted to our Tribe or, Indian Tribes in general. The right to conduct gaming is an inherent power of government. The 1987 United States Supreme Court decision in the *Cabazon* case found that Indian gaming was an exercise and expression of Tribal government and Self-Determination. In *Cabazon*, the Court held that State governments could not impose their regulatory gaming laws to stop Tribal governments from engaging in gaming activities. Following that decision, Congress passed the IGRA in 1988 as a means of providing some Federal guidance on Tribal gaming. IGRA created the National Indian Gaming Commission (NIGC) within the Department, and tasked the Department with some authority to oversee per capita payments (for the Tribes that make those payments from gaming proceeds); as well as review authority for Tribal-State gaming compacts. Very few Tribes provide their Tribal members per capita payments. Jamestown does not provide per capita payments; instead, we invest in opportunities for our members to better their lives through programs that matter and make a difference—education; health; culture; and jobs creating economic development.

The Department also retains authority for regulating gaming on certain lands acquired in trust after Cabazon, as well as approval authority for newly acquired and additional trust lands for gaming. But it must be understood that these roles for the Department were not put in place to create regulatory obstacles to Indian economic development. In each case, the intent behind the Department's role is to maximize the positive benefits of Indian gaming, whether it is for individual Tribal members, or State and Tribal governments. There are many reasons Tribes negotiate in good faith with states to enter into gaming compacts, including, to create meaningful opportunities for economic growth, invest in education and programs and services that promote the health and welfare of our Tribal citizens, create jobs and opportunities, assist in addressing the historic loss of Tribal homelands and to acquire land for economic development.

The current Administration has vowed to thoroughly revamp the Federal regulatory landscape in favor of reducing burdens and limitations on economic development. However, some of the proposed regulatory changes which will in fact increase bureaucratic oversight and create additional burdens for Tribes, are contrary to Self-Governance and Self-Determination, and impose barriers to economic development, investment, and financial self-sufficiency. Tribes have worked hard to encourage the Department to listen to Tribal leaders on how to strike the right balance. In 2016, Tribes spent more than $449 million on Tribal, State and Federal regulations: $336.5 million to fund Tribal Gaming Regulatory Agencies; $90.4 million to reimburse states for State regulatory activities negotiated and agreed to pursuant to Tribal/State compacts; and $22.2 million to fully fund the operations and activities of the National Indian Gaming Commission.

Tribes have a vested interest in protecting the integrity of Indian gaming. Tribal regulation ensures that our communities are shielded from organized crime and other corrupt influences that could infiltrate any economic development activity if left unchecked. Back in the 1990s, the issue of organized crime was alleged but not one case of organized crime has been proven on an Indian reservation. However, there are many factors other than gaming that have attributed to the high incidence of crime in many Tribal communities. The Indian Law and Order Commission, which was established pursuant to the Tribal Law and Order Act, found that a complex jurisdictional scheme, lack of coordination, accountability and adequate and consistent funding resources led to a crisis of crime on Indian reservations that have persisted for decades. It is misleading to equate gaming with the high incidence of crime in Indian country because there are many Tribes who do not have gaming facilities who experience high crime in their communities. In our community, Tribal resources and local collaboration have not only improved the safety and security of our Tribal citizens but also the surrounding local communities. We collect data and submit monthly crime reports to the Department that is reflective of the low incidence of criminal activity in our community. Tribal regulation of gaming also mandates that the Tribal community is the primary beneficiary of gaming, not some outside corporation, and that gaming is fair and honest.

For my Tribe, gaming revenue provides diversification to our local economy, employment opportunities for Tribal and non-Tribal citizens, and funding to provide programs and services to our community including: scholarships and education funding; healthcare/programs for vulnerable citizens like our elders and children; cultural programs that support language, arts, and cultural revitalization; environmental restoration and preservation of our estuaries and resource habitat that supports our fishing industry; and, community and local infrastructure, including, building roads and bridges.

Facts about Indian Gaming

It is extremely important that Congress also understands the national Tribal gaming picture. Not every Indian Tribe has a casino. In 2016, approximately 244 out of 567 Federally-recognized Tribal Governments operated 484 gaming facilities in 28 states for a total of $35.4 billion in revenues. In many cases, due to geographic location and other limiting factors, those revenues are largely covering expenses, paying wages and benefits to employees, and otherwise keeping businesses afloat.

First and foremost, Indian gaming, wherever it is located is about jobs. Many Tribes operate gaming to generate jobs for their Tribal citizens and local community residents. In 2016, Indian gaming generated more than 310,000 direct jobs and when you include indirect jobs nearly 700,000 Americans are employed which is attributable to Indian gaming. Our Tribe is one of the largest employers in our community, which means that a substantial benefit of our Tribe building a diverse economy is that all residents—Indian and non-Indian—benefit through jobs and local economic development business enterprises. Overall, up to 75 percent of the jobs in Tribal casinos go to non-Indian employees, so the income generated by these enterprises has substantial spillover effects for entire regions.

For the gaming Tribes that do generate profits, there are rules about how Tribes may use those funds. What I see when I travel around Indian Country are communities that use gaming profits to improve and build their infrastructures, support educational opportunities and social programs, decrease reliance on public and governmental programs, and create substantial investments in health care systems, jobs creation, and economic sustainability. In addition, lenders, States and Tribes all share in the revenue generated at gaming facilities. Gaming continues to be the most successful tool for economic development.

A fundamental goal for our Tribe is achieving economic self-sufficiency/self-reliance through opportunities that enable us to generate our own unrestricted revenues to address the unfulfilled Federal obligations and unmet needs in our community. Until we achieve tax parity we must rely on other sources of revenue, such as, gaming revenue to support critical governmental services such as police, fire, first responders, education, housing, and healthcare.

In closing, gaming has allowed us to invest in our local community and create sustainable Tribal economies that promote economic development and job creation and contribute to the economic well-being of our Tribal citizens. It has also fortified our partnerships with State and local governments and allowed us to make significant contributions to their economies creating jobs and opportunities for all Americans.

Thank you for the opportunity to submit this testimony.

PREPARED STATEMENT OF KLINT A. COWAN. SHAREHOLDER, FELLERS SNIDER

Dear Mr. Chairman:

My name is Klint A. Cowan. I am a shareholder at Fellers Snider, a law firm in Oklahoma City, Oklahoma. I represent Panhandle Citizens for Truth in Gaming, Inc., a group of Oklahoma citizens from the Oklahoma panhandle.

The purpose of my testimony is to address a substantial issue involving my clients in relation to a proposed off-reservation casino in Guymon, Oklahoma for the Shawnee Tribe of Oklahoma. Currently, the Shawnee Tribe has an applicationl for off-reservation gaming and an application [1] for a land to trust acquisition pending before the United States Department of the Interior (the "Department") in relation to a proposed casino site in Guymon. The Shawnee Tribe is located in Miami, Oklahoma, which is the extreme northeast corner of Oklahoma. This particular proposed casino, if approved, carries the substantial likelihood of detrimentally impacting the State of Oklahoma, as well as any state in the United States, in part, by setting an extremely dangerous precedent with respect to off-reservation gaming. For this reason, as fully described below, I am strongly advocating that clearer guidelines are put in place that will ensure that both the Indian tribe and local governments and communities are mutually benefited by any proposed off-reservation casino to ensure the long-term success and sustainability of off-reservation gaming and the local communities in which the off-reservation casino is located.

Guymon is located in the approximate middle of the Oklahoma panhandle. The distance from the Shawnee Tribe's headquarters in the extreme northeast corner of Oklahoma to Guymon is over four hundred (400) miles. The Shawnee Tribe has no historical or modern connection to the panhandle, and no Shawnee tribal members live in the panhandle. The local governments and communities in the panhandle are strongly opposed to the proposed casino. Thirty-Eight (38) local governmental officials in the panhandle submitted letters of opposition to the Department, while only two (2) governmental officials expressed support. It is especially notable that the Guymon City Council formally voted to oppose the proposed casino, and two (2) of three (3) of the Texas County [2] Commissioners sent letters of opposition. Moreover, in addition to numerous letters of opposition, more than two thousand (2,000) local citizens in the panhandle signed a petition in opposition to the proposed casino. [3] In addition, the Shawnee Tribe has not entered into any agreements with the local governments, or even attempted to negotiate any such agreements, in an attempt to mitigate the adverse effects that a casino will have on the local government budgets, programs and economy.

This particular set of facts carries a very dangerous precedent for the State of Oklahoma, and for any state in our country. In the event that an off-reservation casino is approved at such a substantial distance from a tribe's headquarters, where the tribe has no historical or modern connection whatsoever to the area and the local governments and citizens are strongly opposed to the casino, an off-reservation casino could be justified in virtually any location in the United States. Taking the Shawnee Tribe's applications as an example, the Cities of Omaha, Nebraska; Shreveport, Louisiana; St. Louis, Missouri; and Memphis, Tennessee are closer to the Shawnee Tribe's headquarters than the proposed casino site in Guymon, and would conceivably be in play for a future casino. Much to the contrary, the Shawnee Tribe claims jurisdiction over land in eastern Kansas and has a gaming compact pending with the State of Kansas. This land seems imminently more suitable for off-reservation gaming, as the Tribe has a historical connection to the eastern Kansas area which is much closer to the Tribe's headquarters.

It also must be observed that the Department has a history of relying on precedent to justify off-reservation gaming. For example, in a 2-Part Determination dated August 23, 2013, former Assistant Secretary—Indian Affairs Kevin Washburn approved an off-reservation casino for the Menominee Tribe which was approximately 162 miles from the tribe's governmental headquarters. Assistant Secretary Washburn noted that:

"Admittedly, allowing an off-reservation casino located more than 150 miles from a reservation headquarters might not be appropriate in any other state,

---

[1] The Obama administration approved the off-reservation gaming application at the "midnight hour" on January 19, 2017. Oklahoma Governor Mary Fallin, despite the substantial opposition of the citizens in the panhandle, concurred in the 2-Part Determination on or about March 3, 2017. The land to trust application is currently pending before the Department, and the 2-Part Determination is being reviewed for potential reconsideration.

[2] Guymon is located in Texas County, Oklahoma.

[3] The petition contains an extraordinary number of signatures given the sparse population in the panhandle area.

but the Forest County determination of 1990 is a very specific precedent for such an action in Wisconsin."

The proposed Guymon casino carries the substantial likelihood of serving as precedent to justify an off-reservation casino virtually anywhere.

Clearer guidance is necessary to foster off-reservation gaming that will be mutually beneficial to Indian tribes and to local governments and communities. The Department previously operated under a set of guidelines known as the "Artman Guidelines"[4] which clarified certain regulatory limitations for land-to-trust acquisitions to ensure a mutually beneficial relationship between Indian tribes and local governments and communities. The Artman Guidelines defined an appropriate distance between a tribe's headquarters and the proposed trust acquisition land for the purposes of historical and modern connection and employment of tribal members. Moreover, the Artman Guidelines espoused that Indian tribes execute a memorandum of understanding with the local governments, prior to obtaining approval of the land-to-trust application. In this way, the Indian tribes and local governments would be sure to ameliorate any adverse impacts on the local communities in order to ensure a long-term mutually beneficial and sustainable relationship.

Without clearer guidance limiting Indian tribes' off-reservation gaming activities to areas which are proximately located to the tribe's headquarters, to where the tribe has a historical and modern connection, and to where the Indian tribes and local governments and citizens are committed to working with each other to develop a mutually beneficial and longterm relationship, off-reservation gaming will not achieve optimal levels of success for Indian tribes and the United States. I strongly recommend that this Committee pursue and/or mandate clear guidance to ensure the long-term success and sustainability of off-reservation gaming.

While I am not providing live-testimony to this Committee, I would certainly invite any written or verbal questions and feedback from the Committee members, and will make myself available through any medium necessary. My contact information is provided in my letterhead. Thank you for the opportunity to address this Committee.

RESPONSE TO WRITTEN QUESTIONS SUBMITTED BY HON. JERRY MORAN TO HON. JONODEV OSCEOLA CHAUDHURI

Question 1. Mr. Chaudhuri, in 2008, the National Indian Gaming Commission (NIGC) promulgated technical standards governing Class II gaming machines to ensure their security and integrity. At the time, there were concerns that these particular machines were susceptible to security risks like hacking. Given the prevalence of such risks across society today, is it fair to assume that such risks have increased significantly since 2008? If so, how have those risks changed in recent years?

Answer. As stated in the preamble to the final rule promulgated on October 10, 2008, the Commission developed the minimum technical standards "to ensure the security and integrity of Class II games played with technologic aids, to ensure the auditability of the gaming revenue that those games earn, and to account and allow for evolving and new technology." The Commission developed the technical standards to provide minimum design, construction, and implementation requirements for Class II gaming systems while the companion internal control standards were developed to provide minimum controls for the operation of such systems, as well as the authorization, recognition, and recordation of gaming and gaming-related transactions. Together, the technical standards and internal control standards make meaningful the Commission's monitoring, inspection, and examination authority. These minimum standards further IGRA's goal of ensuring that gaming is conducted fairly and honestly, both by operators and by the public, while leaving specific implementations designed to meet these regulatory goals to the tribal gaming regulatory authorities and industry. The Commission thereby sought to build into the technical standards the flexibility to respond to risks that may change over time and to implement future technologies unforeseen and undeveloped when the rule was first promulgated. Finally, the technical standards expressly provide that they are minimum standards—tribal gaming regulatory authorities may add additional or more stringent requirements for manufacturers to implement before a Class II gaming system may be authorized for use by the tribal gaming operation.

---

[4] The "Artman Guidelines" were officially known as "Guidance on taking off-reservation land into trust for gaming purposes," dated January 3, 2008. Then Assistant Secretary—Indian Affairs, Carl Artman, issued the guidelines.

Question 2. Along these same lines, would such improved standards help preserve the integrity of these Class II machines by minimizing error and variance rates? If so, please explain further. If not, are you of the belief that the older technology provides the same levels of protection against any such errors?

Answer. As noted above, the minimum technical standards were intended to leave the specific implementations of the standards to the tribal gaming regulatory authorities and industry. Thus, rather than requiring the specific use of a particular form of technology, the technical standards require the implementation of certain features which may be implemented by a wide array of technology. For example, the technical standards require components that store financial instruments and that are not operated under the control of a gaming operation employee "shall be located within a secure and locked area or in a locked cabinet or housing that is of a robust construction designed to resist determined illegal entry and to protect internal components." How exactly "robust construction" is to be implemented is left to industry to develop, independent testing laboratories to review, and tribal gaming regulatory authorities and operations to authorize for use. The standard, however, is clear—assets held in gaming equipment are to be secure from theft and tampering.

Question 3. Despite the noticeable need for implementing such security standards for Class II machines in 2008, the NIGC implemented a five-year "grandfather period," temporarily exempting older gaming systems to "avoid any potential significant economic impact" of requiring immediate compliance. Another five-year period was granted again in 2012 and lasts through November of 2018. Given the current positive economic health of Indian gaming, is it fair to state that requiring the implementation of such standards at this time would not cause economic harm to either the tribes or the manufacturers? If not, please elaborate.

Answer. It is important to note that the economic health of Indian gaming as a whole, which includes both Class II and Class III gaming, is not necessarily representative of the economic health of Indian gaming operations that would be affected by changes to the implementation requirements of the Class II minimum technical standards. When the minimum technical standards were implemented in 2008, the Commission recognized that some existing Class II gaming systems did not meet all of the requirements of the technical standards and that requiring immediate compliance could have a significant economic impact. Gaming systems manufactured before the effective date of the Commission's minimum technical standards (2008 Systems) were therefore permitted to continue in operation provided that such systems were submitted to an independent testing laboratory and reviewed for compliance with standards for, among others, random number generation, minimum probabilities, and game software verification. Gaming systems manufactured after the effective date of the Commission's minimum technical standards are required to be submitted to a testing laboratory and reviewed for compliance with all applicable technical standards. In addition, minimum internal control standards apply uniformly to the operation of all Class II gaming systems, irrespective of manufacture date. This year, the Commission consulted extensively with the tribal gaming industry on the continued use of 2008 Systems and received many comments asserting that there was no evidence that such systems posed a threat to the integrity of gaming and that requiring their removal from play would cause significant economic harm to tribes. Subsequently, after conducting an internal analysis of the potential issues associated with the continued use of 2008 Systems, the Commission issued a proposed rule which allows such use provided that the systems are subject to additional annual review by tribal gaming regulatory authorities.

Question 4. By not adopting more modern standards with regard to technology used in Class II machines, do we risk impeding innovation within the Class II gaming manufacturer community? If so, is it fair to say that this lack of innovation negatively impacts the tribes themselves as any potential gamers may stay away due to either security or integrity concerns?

As noted above, the minimum technical standards were intended to leave the specific implementations of the standards to the tribal gaming regulatory authorities and industry. Thus, rather than requiring the specific use of a particular form of technology, the technical standards require the implementation of certain features which may be implemented by a wide array of technology. In addition, the minimum technical standards allow Class II gaming systems to be modified over time as manufacturers innovate new implementations of the required features. Tribes and tribal gaming regulatory authorities may also add additional or more stringent requirements for manufacturers to implement. The technical standards, in conjunction with internal control standards, ensure that security concerns are identified and mitigated, thereby meeting the goal of ensuring that Class II gaming is conducted fairly and honestly, both by operators and by the public.

RESPONSE TO WRITTEN QUESTIONS SUBMITTED BY HON. TOM UDALL TO JOHN TAHSUDA III

Question 1. The Administration recently published an advance notice of proposed rulemaking [1] indicating its intent to revise the off-reservation land into trust process for parcels that could later be eligible for gaming.

Question 1a. In the 29 years since the passage of IGRA, a governor concurred in a positive two part determination only 10 times. And of the over 1,700 successful trust acquisitions processed from 2008 to 2014, fewer than 15 acquisitions were for gaming purposes, with even fewer for off-reservation gaming purposes. What is the Administration's impetus for revising the regulations regarding off-reservation acquisitions?

Answer. As a point of clarification, the Department did not issue an advance notice of proposed rulemaking; rather, on October 4, 2017, the Department distributed a draft of possible revisions to tribal leaders for consultation purposes. The Department withdrew the draft and then sent a revised consultation schedule to tribal leaders on December 6, 2017, with questions for discussion at the consultation sessions. The purpose of the consultation is to clarify the land into trust process and to seek ways to save tribal resources.

With regard to your question, the application process for taking land into trust for gaming purposes can be costly and time consuming, particularly when compared to non-gaming applications. Currently, tribal applicants must submit all the application information, including certain resource-intensive application information, before the Department will consider the trust application. Rather than requiring tribes to expend much-needed resources pursuing a trust acquisition with no certainty of the outcome, the Department is considering ways to revise the existing regulations to reduce the burden on tribal applicants. The Department is also open to considering other revisions to the regulations and the land-into-trust process and criteria and has requested input from tribes for their ideas.

Question 1b. In your written testimony, you noted that gaming can introduce "new complications" to local communities, such as "a drain on local resources" due to crime. Given that IGRA and its implementing regulations already require Interior to conclude that an acquisition would not be detrimental to the surrounding community, how does Interior intend the new regulations to give greater consideration of impacts to communities than the existing requirements?

Answer. Local communities are often in the best position to assess potential impacts from off-reservation gaming that would affect them. Off-reservation lands taken in trust can potentially create jurisdictional impacts in local communities, complicate land-use planning, and affect the provision of local services such as law enforcement. The Department is considering whether the regulations should request evidence of any cooperative efforts to mitigate impacts to the local community, including copies of any intergovernmental agreements negotiated between the Tribe and state and local governments, if any, or an explanation as to why no such agreements or efforts exist. In this way, the Department would be better able to determine potential impacts to the surrounding communities. In practice, tribal applicants often provide information about their cooperative agreements even though it is not specifically required by the existing Part 151 regulations.

Question 1c. The Administration proposes to give greater weight to local concerns the further away the proposed acquisition is from the Tribe's reservation. This seems to be a thumb on the scales in a manner not intended by the statute. What is the Department's reasoning?

Answer. Part 151 currently requires that as the distance between a tribe's reservation and the land to be acquired increases, the Secretary shall give greater scrutiny to the tribe's justification of anticipated benefits from the acquisition, and greater weight to concerns raised by state and local governments as to the acquisition's potential impacts on regulatory jurisdiction, real property taxes, and special assessments. *See* 25 C.F.R. § 151.11(b). The Department is considering whether greater clarity on what factors would provide evidence to support a decision on the relative justifications and concerns would be helpful to the tribe and surrounding communities.

Question 1d. You testified that the Department had not adequately applied the Part 151 regulations in the past few years. Please provide the specific trust acquisitions to which you referred in your testimony where the Department believes it had not previously considered the factors in an adequate manner.

---

[1] Off-Reservation Trust Acquisitions and Action on Trust Acquisition Requests, available at https://www.reginfo.gov/public/do/eAgendaViewRule?pubId=201704&RIN=1076-AF36

Answer. As stated in my verbal response to this question at the oversight hearing on October 4, 2017, "I think that it is our [the Department's] belief that past actions over the years did not adequately apply our regulations as they should have so that all factors and criteria to be adequately considered were not adequately considered. . .some were given greater priority over others."

It is our commitment to consider all the factors we are required to consider by the law and by our regulations and apply those to the factual situation in front of us.

Question 1e. We understand that the Department intends to hold tribal regional consultation sessions on the draft regulations. Will the Department conduct similar consultations once the regulations are formally issued? In other words, will tribes have additional opportunities to comment as the proposal advances toward final?

Answer. On December 6, 2017, the Department advised tribes that it would be consulting on a list of questions related to the fee-to-trust process, and announced six consultations for January and February. The Department will determine next steps following those consultation sessions, in compliance with the Administrative Procedure Act and the Department's consultation policy.

Question 1f. In the draft regulations, Interior proposes a new requirement that a tribe demonstrate a historic or modern connection to the land for off-reservation acquisitions. What is the statutory basis for this requirement?

Answer. Section 5 of the Indian Reorganization Act provides the general authority for the Secretary to acquire land in trust for Tribes. The Secretary has the authority to promulgate regulations, as found in Part 151, to implement the statutory grant of discretionary authority in Section 5.

The draft changes reflect the Department's continued interest in balancing tribal interests. In practice, tribal applicants often provide information on their historic or modern connection to the land even though it is not specifically required by the existing Part 151 regulations.

Question 1g. The last time an administration imposed a "commutability requirement" like the kind reflected in Interior's recently circulated draft—tribes objected on the grounds that such a rule prejudiced tribes with reservations away from population centers and ignored historical facts regarding where the federal government created reservations. What is the Administration's response?

Answer. The draft revisions did not impose a specific distance requirement in recognition that each Tribe's circumstances may differ. Rather, the draft revisions reflected factors, like those in the existing Part 151 regulations, which analyzed the anticipated benefits to the Tribe from the acquisition and the concerns of local governments.

Question 2. The Tenth Circuit recently held that Part 291 is inconsistent with IGRA, leaving tribes in the 10th Circuit without administrative redress if a state decides it does not want to negotiate a compact. If Interior cannot issue Secretarial procedures, what options do tribes have now, given IGRA's intent to give tribes at least some bargaining power relative to the states during the compact negotiation process?

Answer. Tribes are authorized by the "good faith lawsuit" provision of IGRA to file suit against a state that has not negotiated in good faith.[2] A state may, however, raise an Eleventh Amendment defense to such a lawsuit which would then be dismissed due to the non-waiver of the state's sovereign immunity.[3] Secretarial Procedures promulgated pursuant to 25 C.F.R Part 291 would be a Tribe's only other recourse to engage in class III gaming in circuits other than the Tenth and Fifth.[4] In circuits where states have refused to negotiate with Tribes and have invoked their Eleventh Amendment rights, Tribes retain the ability to conduct class II gaming on Indian lands without a tribal-state compact.

Question 3. As a part of the advance notice of proposed rulemaking referenced above, the Administration proposed a 30-day delay before finalizing trust acquisitions. In light of Match-E-Be-Nash-She-Wish Band of Pottawatomi Indians v. Patchak, in which the Supreme Court found that challenges to trust acquisitions are "garden-variety [Administrative Procedure Act] claim[s]" subject to a six-year statute of limitations and preliminary injunctions, what is the purpose of a 30-day stay?

Answer. As a point of clarification, the Department did not issue an advance notice of proposed rulemaking; rather, on October 4, 2017, the Department distributed

---

[2] *See* 25 U.S.C. § 2710 (d)(7)(A)(i).

[3] *See Seminole Tribe of Florida v. Florida,* 517 U.S. 44 (1996). Only California has a waiver of sovereign immunity for tribal-state compacts.

[4] *See Texas v. U.S.,* 497 F.3d 491 (5612007); and *New Mexico v. Zinke,* Nos. 14–2219 # 14–222 (10th April 21,2017).

a draft of revisions to tribal leaders for consultation purposes. The Department then sent a revised consultation schedule to tribal leaders on December 6, 2017, with questions for discussion at the consultation sessions.

With regard to the 30-day stay that was included in the draft revisions distributed October 4, the Department is interested in tribes' input on the stay. Currently, there is no general authority for the executive branch to take lands out of trust. The authority to take trust lands out of trust status rests with Congress and potentially the judicial branch. The draft revisions would reinstate the 30-day waiting period to enable potential litigants to file during that 30-day period before title is transferred into trust. The 30-day waiting period is intended to help prevent situations where title is transferred into trust, and a Tribe expends resources developing that land, only to face protracted litigation and the possibility of having the land be taken out of trust.

Question 4. When an Indian tribe and a state submit a Class III gaming compact or compact amendment to the Secretary for review, Congress authorized the Secretary to take only one of two actions: approve the compact amendment, or disapprove the compact amendment. If the Secretary fails to take either action within 45 days of submittal, Congress mandated that the compact or amendment will be "considered to have been approved," a directive that is also reflected in Interior's regulations. Recently, the Secretary "returned" a compact amendment to the Mohegan Tribe of Connecticut and to the Mashantucket Pequot Tribal Nation of Connecticut, rather than taking action on it.

Question 4a. Can you indicate where in IGRA Congress authorized the Secretary to "return" a submitted compact amendment without triggering IGRA's deemed approved requirement?

Answer. The Department did not act on the proposed compact amendments because there was insufficient information to determine whether they fell within the Secretary's jurisdiction pursuant to IGRA and whether the Secretary had authority to approve or disapprove them.

Question 4b. Given that the compact amendment is now deemed approved by operation of IGRA and its implementing regulations, when will the Secretary publish notice of the approval in the Federal Register?

Answer. The Department did not have sufficient information to determine whether the proposed compact amendments fell within the Secretary's statutory authority pursuant to IGRA. The Department specifically rejected the deemed approved option, therefore there are no plans to publish a notice of approval in the Federal Register for the proposed compact amendments.

○

www.ingramcontent.com/pod-product-compliance
Lightning Source LLC
Chambersburg PA
CBHW060003230526
45472CB00008B/1924